ONE DAY
CELESTIAL NAVIGATION

For Offshore Sailing

Otis S. Brown

Published by:
C & O Research
4409 Cape Cod Circle
Bowie, Maryland 20715

Distributed by:
Liberty Publishing Company, Inc.
50 Scott Adam Road
Cockeysville, Maryland 21030

First Edition 1979
Second Edition 1981
Third Edition 1984
Fourth Edition 1988

Library of Congress #79-67243
ISBN #0-89709-132-9

Cover by Art Etris

The author thanks the following people
for their assistance: Carol Brown,
Helen Jones and Vera Rollo.

Manufactured USA

To
Sherm & Marian Brown

INTRODUCTION

This book is designed for the individual with no experience in celestial navigation. It takes you from elementary shots to sophisticated shots where you check the accuracy of the ship's compass at sea. If you have enough experience to navigate yourself out of the harbor, this book will find you your island.

There are a number of texts available on celestial navigation, most of which are all-or-nothing. Either you follow the entire procedure or you are lost. Small errors are difficult to find and cause serious problems and befuddlement. These texts tend to have incomprehensible or nonexistent work forms. This course is designed to give you immediate capability with a sextant. The simple part of celestial navigation is taught in the first two chapters. At this point you will have found your latitude and double checked it.

Finding your latitude by Chapter One is sufficient to find your island. You may have to "dog leg" down to it, but an accurate latitude will give you an accurate landfall. The simple longitude check (in Chapter Two) will tell you how far you are from your island. You may wish to stop at this point if these two chapters meet your navigational needs.

If you desire full competency with celestial navigation you must read Chapter Three, *The Longitude Shot*. You may then execute an afternoon shot and plot your position. Chapter Four covers special techniques and qualifies you as a competent navigator.

This book looks at celestial navigation through the eyes of the beginner. Every procedure has an independent double check. If you correctly calculate your latitude in Chapter One, it will match the latitude check in Chapter Two. If you correctly calculate your longitude in Chapter Three it will match the simple longitude check in Chapter Two. Chapter Four demonstrates a triple shot technique to confirm the accuracy of all three Lines of Position.

Crossing sun Lines of Position will meet all your navigational needs. After you have become expert with sun navigation you may wish to continue with other celestial objects. Slight modifications to the work form in Chapter Five will give you full capability with the Moon, Stars and Planets.

How much you accomplish in celestial navigation depends on *you!*

CONTENTS

CHAPTER I

THE LATITUDE SHOT

Celestial navigation has a reputation for being complex. Nothing could be further from the truth! If you can add and subtract, you can learn this navigation technique. The total cost of the required materials is (including the sextant) less than $100.

An emergency is defined as a sudden or unexpected occurrence that demands prompt action. Such an emergency could occur if the navigator is incapacitated. This book is designed to help you out of such a dilemma. But first, take an inventory of your navigation equipment, You need:

1. A Sextant
2. A Nautical Almanac
3. An accurate watch
4. HO 249. (Two books of tables cover-latitudes 0 – 40 degrees and 40 – 89 degrees, Volumes II and III)

Don't panic if you don't have all these items. Chapter I tells you how to find your way back to port with *only a sextant and a Nautical Almanac.*

Now for your problem. You are faced with an endless horizon and have only a hazy idea of where you are. Get out the map of the port you left several days ago. What is the latitude and longitude of the port? Knowing the direction and speed you have been sailing, you should be able to make an estimate of your position. The procedure given here will yield an accurate latitude even with considerable error in your estimated position.

You will begin with the simplest of shots – – the high noon, or latitude shot. Read this chapter, work the example problems and then shoot the sun at high noon. It will give you an accurate latitude.

Now, let's go to sea!

You are sailing with me off the coast of Carolina. It is mid-morning on Monday, June 22, 1987. Your approximate position is N 32°02′ and W 79°23′.

WHEN DO I SHOOT?

To obtain your latitude you must shoot the sun at high noon. This normally is not 12 o'clock, but must be calculated by using the Nautical Almanac. You start by filling in your work sheet with the day of the week and the date. Round off your latitude and longitude to the nearest whole degree and enter it in the log.   (Page 11)

Next, under *PREDICTING HIGH NOON,* calculate the GMT (Greenwich Mean Time) that high noon occurs for your position. Turn to the daily pages of the Nautical Almanac. Looking on the lower right hand side of the page you find the meridian pass which is 12:02.   (See overleaf)

Enter this in your work sheet.

> MERIDIAN PASS 12:02
> LONGITUDE W 79 . . . 5:16 (Add if West)
> _____
> GMT OF NOON . . . . . 17:18 (Total)

You know the "meridian pass" for zero degrees longitude. What is the meridian pass at W 79? How long does it take for the earth to turn through an angle of 79 degrees? You must convert 79 degrees into an equivalent time. Turn to the start of the yellow pages in the back of the Nautical Almanac. The table is labeled *CONVERSION OF ARC TO TIME.* You can see that 79 degrees equals 5 hours and 16 minutes. Since you are west, you will add your time to the meridian pass. The result, 17 hours and 18 minutes, is the GMT that high noon occurs for your longitude.

HOW HIGH WILL THE SUN BE?

Turning back to the daily page, look up the declination (Dec.) of the sun for 17:00 hours. This value, N $23°26'$, is entered in the work sheet. (Round off 26.5' to 26'. If your time is greater than 17:31, use the declination for the next highest hour.)

Now, calculate the height of the sun at your assumed latitude; 32 degrees north. Enter your latitude under *PREDICTING HEIGHT OF SUN.* Subtract 32 degrees from 90 degrees. The result is 58 degrees. This is the height of the celestial equator above the southern horizon. The celestial equator, in this application, is a reference value. If the sun's declination is zero degrees, the sun's height will be 58 degrees. If the sun's declination is not zero, you will add or subtract the sun's declination from 58 degrees. (See work form Page 11)

22	00	179 33.9	N23	26.6
	01	194 33.8		26.6
	02	209 33.6		26.6
	03	224 33.5	. .	26.6
	04	239 33.4		26.6
	05	254 33.2		26.6
	06	269 33.1	N23	26.6
	07	284 32.9		26.6
	08	299 32.8		26.5
M	09	314 32.7	. .	26.5
O	10	329 32.5		26.5
N	11	344 32.4		26.5
D	12	359 32.3	N23	26.5
A	13	14 32.1		26.5
Y	14	29 32.0		26.5
	15	44 31.9	. .	26.5
	16	59 31.7		26.5
	17	74 31.6		26.5
	18	89 31.4	N23	26.4
	19	104 31.3		26.4
	20	119 31.2		26.4
	21	134 31.0	. .	26.4
	22	149 30.9		26.4
	23	164 30.8		26.4

1987 JUNE 21, 22, 23

DAILY PAGE

MERIDIAN PASS

	SUN		
Day	Eqn. of Time		Mer.
	00 h	12 h	Pass.
	m s	m s	h m
21	01 31	01 38	12 02
22	01 44	01 51	12 02
23	01 57	02 04	12 02

YELLOW PAGE

CONVERSION OF ARC TO TIME

0°–59°			60°–119°			120°–179°			180°–239°		
°	h	m	°	h	m	°	h	m	°	h	m
0	0	00	60	4	00	120	8	00	180	12	00
1	0	04	61	4	04	121	8	04	181	12	04
2	0	08	62	4	08	122	8	08	182	12	08
3	0	12	63	4	12	123	8	12	183	12	12
4	0	16	64	4	16	124	8	16	184	12	16
15	1	00	75	5	00	135	9	00	195	13	00
16	1	04	76	5	04	136	9	04	196	13	04
17	1	08	77	5	08	137	9	08	197	13	08
18	1	12	78	5	12	138	9	12	198	13	12
19	1	16	79	5	16	139	9	16	199	13	16
20	1	20	80	5	20	140	9	20	200	13	20

The note in the work form states "add the Dec. if it is north". You add N 23°26' to 58 degrees. The result, 81°26', is the exact height of the sun at latitude N 32°00'. This is called your calculated height, Hc.

		90°	
LATITUDE		32°	(Subtract)
		58°	(Celestial Equator)
DECLINATION	N	23°26'	(Add Dec. if north)
		81°26'	Calculated height, Hc

WHAT CORRECTIONS DO I APPLY TO MY SEXTANT READINGS?

Index Error

Next, get your sextant and check it for any index error it might have. The index error is the error that occurs because the sextant is not properly zeroed. It is normally measured and removed mathematically. You measure the error this way: Move the "arm" of the sextant until it points to zero degrees, zero minutes; then observe the horizon through the sextant. You will see a real and a reflected horizon. Move the arm until the horizons overlap. Reading the sextant, you find that it is indicating 13' "on arc". This will cause any readings you may make to be 13' higher than the actual altitude. Subtract your index error is you have an "on arc" condition.

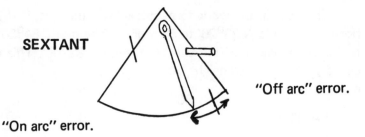

SEXTANT

"Off arc" error.

"On arc" error.

Three additional corrections must be applied to the raw sextant value. They are:

1. Height of eye. (Dip)
2. Semi–diameter. (Same as sun's radius.)
3. Refraction.

These corrections are found on the inside cover of the Nautical Almanac under the title "ALTITUDE CORRECTION TABLES 10° - 90°."

HEIGHT OF EYE

On a small boat your height of eye is approximately 9 feet. This height of eye requires a -3' correction. (See next page.)

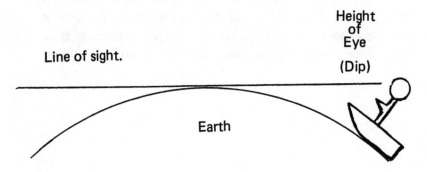

Height
of
Eye

Line of sight.

(Dip)

Earth

ALTITUDE CORRECTION TABLES 10°-90°

SUN APR.—SEPT.		
App. Alt.	Lower Limb	Upper Limb
57 02	−15·4	− 16·4
61 51	−15·5	− 16·3
67 17	−15·6	− 16·2
73 16	−15·7	− 16·1
79 43	−15·8	− 16·0
86 32	−15·9	− 15·9
90 00		

DIP				
Ht. of Eye	Corrⁿ	Ht. of Eye	Ht. of Eye	Corrⁿ
m		ft.	m	
2·4	−2·8	8·0	1·0	− 1·8
2·6	−2·9	8·6	1·5	− 2·2
2·8	−3·0	9·2	2·0	− 2·5
3·0	−3·1	9·8	2·5	− 2·8
3·2	−3·2	10·5	3·0	− 3·0
3·4	−3·3	11·2	See table
3·6		11·9	←

THE EARTH'S ATMOSPHERE BENDS LIGHT FROM THE SUN

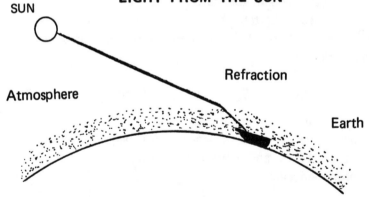

THE SUN'S SEMI-DIAMETER VALUE IS 16′

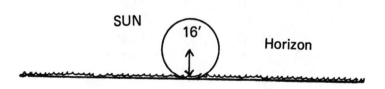

REFRACTION

The sun's rays are bent as they enter the earth's atmosphere. At an angle of 40 degrees, the sun's rays are bent about 1' of angle. At higher altitudes the sun's rays are bent less than this figure.

SEMI-DIAMETER

The sun's semi-diameter value is 16'. When you shoot the sun you bring the sun down until it apparently rests on the horizon. (The lower part of the sun is called the lower limb.) This is the standard procedure for shooting the sun. The 16' of angle is removed by correcting your sextant reading.

In the Nautical Almanac the refraction value is combined with the semi-diameter value. Your calculated height is 81 degrees. The table gives a semi-diameter and refraction value of 15.8' which is rounded off to 16' and entered in the work form.

WHAT DO MY SEXTANT READINGS TELL ME?

It is a good idea to start shooting the sun 20 minutes prior to the expected high noon. You begin recording your shots at 17:14 and continue shooting until 17:22. Your measurements are:

GMT	SEXTANT
17:14	81° 07'
17:16	81° 09'
17:18	81° 10'
17:20	81° 09'
17:22	81° 07'

SUN'S MOTION AT HIGH NOON

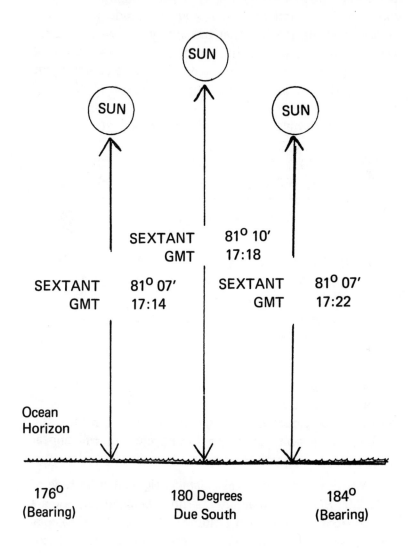

The fact that your measurements peaked near your estimated high noon directly confirms your longitude - - and your GMT calculations. While your longitude verification cannot be exact, the fact that the sun peaked when you expected it to gives you confidence that you are near West 79 degrees. Enter 81° 10′ in the work form and complete the calculations.

```
SEXTANT ................ 81° 10′
INDEX ERROR ...........    - 13′
HEIGHT OF EYE .........    -  3′
SD & REFRACTION ........      16′
────────────────────────────────
OBSERVED HEIGHT ....... 81° 10′  (Total)
```

HOW DO MY OBSERVED AND CALCULATED HEIGHTS DETERMINE MY LATITUDE?

As you shoot the sun, be aware that you are looking almost due south, by reference to your magnetic compass. The sun passed to the south of your position.

For the purpose of visualization, assume that the sun is on top of a 10,000 mile tall tower. If you were at the base of the tower you would look straight up, 90° 00′ to see the sun. As you move away from the tower, the sun will appear lower and lower on your horizon.

You know the sun's calculated height at a latitude of N 32°00′. Since you measure the sun as being lower, you are farther from the sun than latitude N 32°00′. Your calculations show a 16′ difference between your observed height and your calculated height.

THE LATITUDE SHOT

Date _June 22, 1987_   Day _Monday_
Latitude: _N 32°_   Longitude _W 79°_

PREDICTING HIGH NOON

Meridian Pass . . . .   _12:02_
Longitude: _W 79°_   (Add time if west)   _+ 5:16_
                        Sub. time if east

This is the GMT of High Noon: _17:18_
Convert to Local Time: _– 4:00_
This is the local time of High Noon   _13:18_

PREDICTING "HEIGHT OF SUN"

90°   Degrees
LATITUDE: _–32°_   (Subtract)
_58°_   Height of Celestial Equator
(Add Dec. if north)
DECLINATION: _N 23°26'_ Subtract Dec. if south (1)

_81°26'_   Calculated Height (Hc) (2)

SEXTANT MEASUREMENTS

SEXTANT READING . . . .   _81°10'_
(Subtract if "ON ARC")   _– 13'_
INDEX ERROR: Add if "OFF ARC"
HEIGHT OF EYE (DIP) . . . .   _– 3'_
SEMI-DIAMETER AND REFRACTION . . . .   _+ 16'_
TOTAL: OBSERVED HEIGHT (Ho)   _81°10'_

Ho & Hc Comparison
Hc = _81° 26'_
Ho = _81° 10'_   Towards
Ho Mo To   _16'_   (Away) (Difference)

1. If south of equator; add Dec. if south, subtract if north.
2. If Hc is greater than 90°, subtract from 180°.

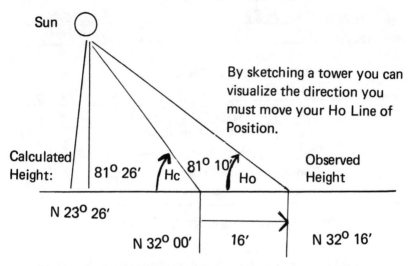

By sketching a tower you can visualize the direction you must move your Ho Line of Position.

Your calculated height is larger than your observed height. You are, therefore, farther away from the tower than N 32° 00'.

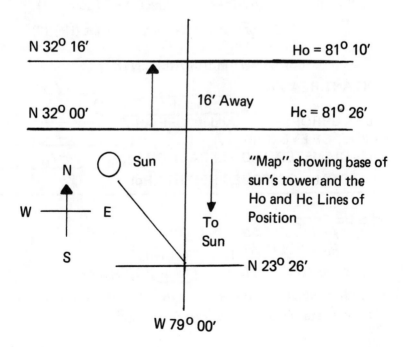

"Map" showing base of sun's tower and the Ho and Hc Lines of Position

Since the top of the tower is 16' lower at your observed position than it is at your calculated position, you must be 16' farther away from the base of the sun's tower.

Ho & Hc Comparison

Calculated Height	81° 26'
Observed Height	81° 10'

		Towards
Ho Mo To	(Difference)	16' (Away)

WHAT IS MY LATITUDE?

Remember the word HoMoTo. This will remind you in which direction you must move your Ho line of position. If *Ho* is *Mo*re than Hc, plot *To*wards the sun. Since this is not true, you will plot your Ho line of position 16' *away* from the sun.

Since the base of the tower is due south, you must be 16' away, or 16 miles north of latitude N 32° 00'. Sketching a map, you draw a line 16 miles north of latitude 32° 00'. *This line is your latitude:* N 32° 16'.

Ho LINE OF POSITION

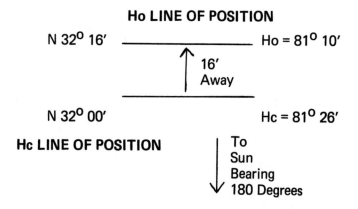

N 32° 16' _____ Ho = 81° 10'

↑ 16'
Away

N 32° 00'   Hc = 81° 26'

Hc LINE OF POSITION   To
Sun
Bearing
↓ 180 Degrees

SUMMARY

The preceding probably seems rather involved. However, since you will be doing this procedure *every day you are at sea,* it will become second nature to you. With practice, the calculation of time of high noon takes little more than a glance at the Nautical Almanac and a quick calculation on a scrap of paper. After you shoot the sun, determining your latitude takes no more than a minute or two.

The advantage of this procedure is its immediate applicability. It gets you thoroughly familiar with the terminology and concepts used in celestial navigation, while at the same time being immediately useful. The methods you learn in this section will enable you to quickly grasp the more difficult techniques presented in Chapter III.

The above method allows you to set your sextant to the sun's height prior to the shot. It allows you to be fully prepared to shoot the sun, and to have a good handle on the required sextant corrections. Finding your latitude is simply a matter of determining the difference between your calculated height and your observed height, and then sketching a "map".

DEFINITION OF TERMS - PART 1

DECLINATION Similar to latitude. This indicates how far — north or south — the sun is from the equator.

GMT Greenwich Mean Time. This is "Earth Standard Time". Celestial navigation requires the use of GMT. This is the correct time at zero degrees longitude.

HIGH NOON This is the time that the sun is highest in the sky. The sun will always be due north or due south at high noon.

Ho Observed Height. This is the height of the sun, after corrections, at *your* position.

Hc Calculated Height. This is the exact height of the sun at your *assumed* position.

LATITUDE Horizontal lines on the map, labeled North and South. Latitude 0 degrees is the equator, and latitude 90 degrees is the north pole. One degree of latitude equals 60 nautical miles.

LONGITUDE Vertical lines on the map, labeled East -and West. Zero degrees passes through Greenwich, England.

LOP Line of Position. You establish a line of position with your observation of the sun. The line of position will run at right angles from the bearing to the sun. If the sun is due south, the sun's line of position will run east and west.

MILE One nautical mile equals 6,080 feet. It is slightly longer than a statute mile. One minute of angle on the earth's surface equals one nautical mile.

PRACTICE   The high noon shot is an excellent way to develop skill with a sextant. The sun will not change its height by more than 2' of angle for a period of 8 minutes of time. (Four minutes before and four minutes after high noon.) Shoot repeatedly during this interval. Your readings should vary no more than three to four minutes of angle. (This non-changing height condition will be true for all sun's heights of less than 80 degrees.)

REDUNDANCY   If you have a friend aboard, both of you should shoot the sun and reduce the shot. If you come up with the same number, you will have a high confidence in the accuracy of your latitude.

SEXTANT   An angle measuring device. An inexpensive model sells for $33. A simple-to-use model which does not require the use of a vernier sells for about $88.

STANDARD   Values. Some values need not be looked up for every shot. On a small boat the standard value for the "Height of Eye" is – 3'. *For the noon shot* the SD & refraction value is 15' or 16'.

SUBTRACTION   Subtract 59°22' from 60°00'. In order to do this you must first subtract 1 degree from 60 degrees and add 60 minutes to 00 minutes.

$$\begin{array}{r} 60^\circ\ 00' \\ -\ 59^\circ\ 22' \\ \hline ?\quad ? \end{array} = \begin{array}{r} 59^\circ\ 60' \\ -\ 59^\circ\ 22' \\ \hline 38' \end{array}$$

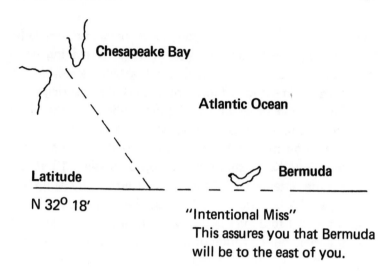

"Intentional Miss"
This assures you that Bermuda
will be to the east of you.

STRATEGY   If you can *only* obtain an accurate latitude, you must modify the approach to your island.
You sail down (or up) to the latitude of the island.
You intentionally miss it to the west (or east) by sixty
miles. This is a dog leg, or "landfall" technique. Upon
arrival at the island's latitude you will know in which
direction to turn to arrive at the island. You will not
know exactly how far you are from the island, but you
will be *certain to hit the island.*

TIME   24 hour time. To simplify calculation,
GMT is kept on the basis of 24 hours to a day. Since
most watches keep time on the basis of 12 hours, it is
necessary to convert watch time to 24 hour time. The
morning hours are read directly; for example, 8 o'clock
is read eight hundred hours. You add 12 hours to the
afternoon hours. Thus, one o'clock in the afternoon is
read as 13 hundred hours.

NO   Time. Should your watch break, or your radio fail, you may continue your voyage by making noon shots. You can use this method without knowing the correct time and without any means of measuring time. Follow the procedure as before, filling out the work form as required. Since you will not know your correct time, you must begin your shots in the middle of the morning. Keep shooting at approximately 10 to 20 minute intervals. Your shots will eventually approach a peak. When they do, increase the frequency of your shots to 1 to 2 minute intervals. Once you have detected the maximum altitude of the sun, you will use this value as your high noon measurement, completing the work form and obtaining your latitude.

HOW DO I CONVERT GMT TO LOCAL TIME?

You know that high noon will occur at GMT 17:18. If you wish to keep local time, you must subtract 4 hours from GMT.

$$
\begin{array}{r}
17:18 \\
-\ 4:00 \\
\hline
13:18
\end{array}
$$

High noon will occur at 13:18 hours, or 1:18 PM Eastern Daylight Time. (See next page)

If you incorrectly calculate local time, it will become apparent to you when you execute your shot of the sun. If you make this error, high noon will occur *one hour* earlier or later than expected.

TABLE FOR CONVERTING GMT TO LOCAL TIME
(Complete tables for local time are listed in the Nautical Almanac)

GMT	Subtract 5 Hours	Eastern Standard Time
GMT	Subtract 6 Hours	Central Standard Time
GMT	Subtract 7 Hours	Mountain Standard Time
GMT	Subtract 8 Hours	Pacific Standard Time

DAYLIGHT SAVING TIME (First Sunday in April until Last Sunday in October.)

GMT	Subtract 4 Hours	Eastern Daylight Time
GMT	Subtract 5 Hours	Central Daylight Time
GMT	Subtract 6 Hours	Mountain Daylight Time
GMT	Subtract 7 Hours	Pacific Daylight Time

TABLE FOR CONVERTING WATCH TIME TO 24 HOUR TIME

24 HOUR	WATCH	24 HOUR	WATCH
00:00	12:00 AM	12:00	12:00 PM
01:00	1:00 AM	13:00	1:00 PM
02:00	2:00 AM	14:00	2:00 PM
03:00	3:00 AM	15:00	3:00 PM
04:00	4:00 AM	16:00	4:00 PM
05:00	5:00 AM	17:00	5:00 PM
06:00	6:00 AM	18:00	6:00 PM
07:00	7:00 AM	19:00	7:00 PM
08:00	8:00 AM	20:00	8:00 PM
09:00	9:00 AM	21:00	9:00 PM
10:00	10:00 AM	22:00	10:00 PM
11:00	11:00 AM	23:00	11:00 PM

PRACTICE PROBLEM

Your responsibility, as captain and navigator of the ship "Capricorn", is to take your vessel from the Chesapeake Bay (N 37° 00' – W 76° 00'), to Bermuda (N 32° 16' – W 64° 50'). You depart the Chesapeake Bay on the morning of June 17, this year. You pick up a heading of 135 degrees true, at a speed of 5 knots. (Five nautical miles per hour.) At noon you shoot the sun to check your ability to obtain your correct latitude. Three days later, having reached the latitude of Bermuda, you turn due east and make a landfall at sunset on June 22. Based on your speed of 5 knots, on a bearing of 135° and 90°, you estimate your noon positions.

You obtain the following measurements:

			Estimated	
	Date	Sextant	Latitude	Longitude
Depart:	June 17	76° 30'	N 37° 00'	W 76° 00'
	June 18	78° 00'	N 35° 20'	W 74° 00'
	June 19	79° 30'	N 34° 00'	W 72° 00'
Turn East:	June 20	81° 00'	N 32° 00'	W 70° 00'
	June 21	81° 09'	N 32° 00'	W 68° 00'
Last Day:	June 22	81° 10'	N 32° 00'	W 66° 00'

Using this year's Nautical Almanac, calculate and plot your noon latitude for June 21. Your height of eye is 9 feet and your sextant's measured index error is 13', "on arc".

(Answers on page 123.)

THE LATITUDE SHOT

Date _____   Day _____
Latitude:_____   Longitude _____

PREDICTING HIGH NOON

Meridian Pass . . . .   _____
Longitude: _____   Add time if west   _____
                                Sub. time if east   _____

    This is the GMT of High Noon: _____
    Convert to Local Time: _____
    This is the local time of High Noon

PREDICTING "HEIGHT OF SUN"

$90°$ Degrees
LATITUDE: _____   (Subtract)

Height of Celestial Equator
Add Dec. if north
DECLINATION: _____ Subtract Dec. if south (1)

Calculated Height (Hc) (2)

SEXTANT MEASUREMENTS

SEXTANT READING . . . .   _____
                        Subtract if "ON ARC"
INDEX ERROR: Add if "OFF ARC"   _____
HEIGHT OF EYE (DIP) . . . .   _____
SEMI-DIAMETER AND REFRACTION . . . .   _____
    TOTAL: OBSERVED HEIGHT (Ho)

Ho & Hc Comparison

_____   Towards
Ho Mo To   Away (Difference)

1. If south of equator; add Dec. if south, subtract if north.
2. If Hc is greater than $90°$, subtract from $180°$.

WORK FORM FOOTNOTES

Footnote #1 is self-explanatory. (If you are south of the equator, reverse this statement. Add the declination if it is south; subtract the declination if it is north).

Footnote #2 is not required if you are north of N 24°, or south of S 24°. If you are between these latitudes, your calculated height will occasionally be greater than 90 degrees. To obtain a calculated height within the range of 0 to 90 degrees, simply subtract your calculated height from 180 degrees.

EXAMPLE

Latitude: N 3° 00'   Sun's Declination: N 23° 00'

Latitude:

$$90^o$$
$$3^o \text{ (Subtract)}$$
―――――

87° (Height of Celestial Equator)
23° 00' (Add if North)
―――――

110° 00' Calculated Height
(which is greater than 90°)

FOOTNOTE #2

180° 00'
- 110° 00'
―――――

70° 00' Calculated Height

CHAPTER II
SHOOTING THE SUN

Now that you have worked out the high noon shot, you are ready for an actual shot. Calculate the time that high noon will occur for *you*, and the sun's expected height. It would be a good idea to have your sextant in your hands as you read this section. I will describe the use of an EBBCO sextant — although the description will fit almost all sextants. * (See next page)

A sextant consists of a body and a moveable arm which swings in an arc. Two mirrors are mounted on the sextant; one on the arm and the other on the body. A telescope is mounted on the body of the sextant and is used to view the horizon, and the sun's reflection. Shades are provided to reduce the intensity of the sun's light.

The arc of the sextant is marked off in degrees. A drum is mounted on the arm of the sextant and allows fine adjustment of the arm. The drum is marked in minutes of angle. This subdivides the degree scale on the body of the sextant.

Prior to making your high noon shot, you must determine the instrument, or index error. Adjust the sextant so it is reading zero degrees and zero minutes. Now look at the horizon through the telescope. If you see one continuous line, the index error is zero.

---

* Read the manual supplied with *your* sextant.

If you see two lines, you have some index error. Adjust the drum of the sextant until the horizon forms a continuous line. Now, read the sextant. If your adjustment caused the arm to move forward, or on to the arc of the sextant, then you have an "on arc" index error. If the arm of the sextant moves towards you, it will be an "off arc" index error, and will be recorded as such in the work form. A little care is required when reading the sextant in the "off arc" condition. As you go below "zero", the sextant would read 50', 40', 30' and so forth. A sextant that indicates 50', and is "off arc", is actually reading 10' below zero, and 10' is the "off arc" value.

The predicted time of your shot was GMT 17:18, and an EDT of 13:18. Since this is your first shot, you will begin shooting the sun 20 minutes early. Set your sextant using the calculated height. (Set your sun shade; as necessary.) Now, look at the horizon in the direction of the sun. The sun will hit you in the eye! Adjust the arm of the sextant until the sun just rests on, or kisses the horizon. (This is called the "lower limb".) Now, sweep the sextant from left to right. The sun will move along the horizon in an arc. You will have to do this to see what I mean. You must adjust your sextant while "swinging" the sextant so the sun just touches the horizon at the lowest point in its travel. (Next page)

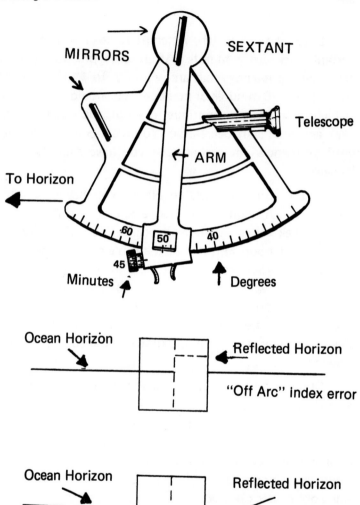

The view of the horizon as seen through the telescope of the Sextant. The arm is set for 0 degrees and 0 minutes.

Look at your watch. Attempt to read and record the sextant once every minute. After some practice, you will begin getting readings that are within 2' to 4' of each other. After about 20 minutes of practice, you should catch the sun at high noon. As you continue to shoot, the readings should peak and then start decreasing. You must continue to shoot until you know for certain that you have shot the sun at its peak.

If the sun continues to climb, you have incorrectly calculated high noon. If this happens, continue shooting and use the peak value, whenever it occurs. You will still obtain your correct noon latitude. If the sun's height is decreasing as you begin your readings, you have made a muck of it and will have to wait until tomorrow to make your latitude shot. Enter your peak value in the log and complete your calculations as previously described. It is a good idea to again check the index error after you have completed your shooting sequence.

Obtaining your latitude via the noon sight — particularly if your friend has shot the sun and gotten the same result — will give you high confidence in your ability and in the accuracy of your latitude. As previously described, getting a correct latitude gives you the capability of getting to your island. No amount of verbiage can substitute for your practicing on the deck of *your* boat with *your* sextant.

SUN'S DISK AS SEEN THROUGH THE SEXTANT

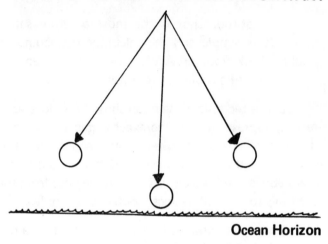

Ocean Horizon

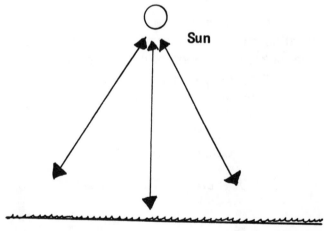

Ocean Horizon

Canting the sextant results in an incorrect height. "Swinging" the sextant assures you that you are reading the correct, or perpendicular, value.

A SIMPLE LATITUDE CHECK

The latitude shot is the most accurate shot you can make. It is simple and the calculations uncomplicated. To double check your previous work, I will present an alternative method of calculating your noon latitude.

Let us reconsider the noon shot. What does your sextant reading represent? It is the exact distance between *you* and the base of the sun's tower — subtracted from 90 degrees. This is called a "complement". If the sun's height is 80 degrees above the horizon, you are 10 degrees from the base of the sun's tower. (10 degrees = 600 nautical miles.)

Since your observed height is 81° 10', the distance to the tower is 90° - 81° 10' = 8° 50'.

Your final goal is to know the distance between your position and the equator. The Nautical Almanac gives you the sun's distance north of the equator as N 23° 26'. You are this distance north of the equator *plus* the distance measured with the sextant:

$$8^O\ 50'\ +\ N\ 23^O\ 26'\ =\ N\ 32^O\ 16'$$
(Ho Complement) (Sun's Dec.)   (Your Latitude)

YOUR LATITUDE IS: N 32° 16'

THE SUMMER SUN

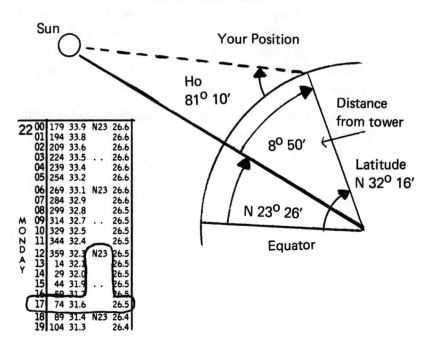

22	00	179 33.9	N23 26.6	
	01	194 33.8		26.6
	02	209 33.6		26.6
	03	224 33.5	..	26.6
	04	239 33.4		26.6
	05	254 33.2		26.6
	06	269 33.1	N23 26.6
	07	284 32.9		26.6
	08	299 32.8		26.5
M	09	314 32.7	..	26.5
O	10	329 32.5		26.5
N	11	344 32.4		26.5
D	12	359 32.3	N23 26.5
A	13	14 32.1		26.5
Y	14	29 32.0		26.5
	15	44 31.9	..	26.5
	16	59 31.7		26.5
	17	74 31.6		26.5
	18	89 31.4	N23 26.4
	19	104 31.3		26.4

A SIMPLE LATITUDE CHECK

$$90^\circ \ 00' \ = \ 89^\circ \quad 60'$$

Observed Height = $81^\circ \quad 10'$

(Subtract)

Distance from tower = $8^\circ \quad 50'$

Sun's Declination = $23^\circ \quad 26'$ (Add in Summer)

(Subtract in Winter)

YOUR LATITUDE IS: $N \ 31^\circ \ 76' \ = \ N \ 32^\circ 16'$

How do you know if you must add or subtract the sun's declination? Simple! Is it winter or summer? In summer the sun is on your side of the equator and you must add the sun's declination to your Ho complement. In winter the sun is on the opposite side of the equator, and you must subtract the sun's declination from the Ho complement.

The sun crosses the equator on March 21, (going north) and on September 21 (going south).

You must be certain to sketch the actual situation to correctly combine the Ho complement with the declination of the sun.

For example, let's look at the case of the "winter" sun. In this example, the sun's tower will be farther away than the equator. The rule for the winter sun requires that you subtract the sun's declination from the Ho complement. (See next page.)

$$55^\circ\ 42' \quad - \quad S\ 23^\circ\ 26' \quad = \quad N\ 32^\circ\ 16'$$
(Ho Complement)   (Sun's Dec.)   (Your Latitude)

THE WINTER SUN

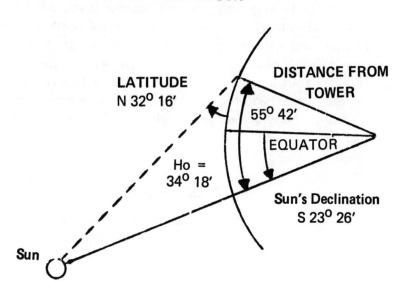

A SIMPLE LATITUDE CHECK

90° 00' = 89° 60'

Observed Height = *34° 18'*

(Subtract)

Distance from tower = *55° 42'*

Sun's Declination = *23° 26'* (Add in Summer)

(Subtract in Winter)

YOUR LATITUDE IS: *N32° 16'*

The last case will occur if you are between the sun's tower and the equator. This condition should be obvious as you will be looking away from the equator as you shoot the sun. (You will be looking north if you are north of the equator, and south if you are south of the equator.) In this case the sun's declination will be a larger number than your latitude. Your latitude will be the difference between your Ho complement and the declination. The illustration on the next page shows the actual situation and the required subtraction.

PRACTICE PROBLEM

You have already calculated your noon latitude for your voyage to Bermuda. Now, use the simple latitude calculation to check your noon shot. (Page 39)

THE SUMMER SUN, SHOT FROM THE TROPICS

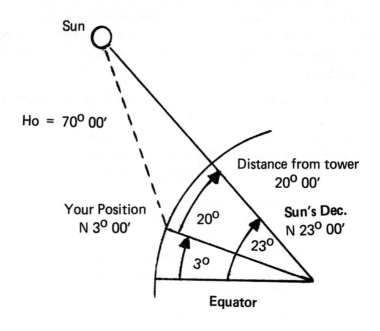

A SIMPLE LATITUDE CHECK

90° 00'	=	90°	00'
Observed Height	=	*70°*	*00'*
			(Subtract)
Distance from tower	=	*20°*	*00'*
Sun's Declination	=	*23°*	*00'*
YOUR LATITUDE IS:		*N 3°*	*00'* (Difference)

A SIMPLE LONGITUDE CHECK

Since the sun crosses your longitude at the same time it peaks, you can determine your longitude if you can determine this point. Unfortunately, you cannot pinpoint the occurrence of high noon with a few shots as the sun "hangs" in the sky.

There is a simple way of measuring the occurrence of high noon. Note that the sun travels in an arc. Note also that this arc is symmetrical with respect to the high noon point. You can make use of this fact to determine the time that noon actually occurred and, thereby, your actual longitude.

For example, let us look at the high noon shot predictions. Your estimated longitude was W 79° 00'. The time of high noon at that longitude is 13:18 EDT. If you shot the sun one hour before and after noon and read 74° 00', you would have confirmed your predicted and actual longitude as being W 79° 00'. (Next page.)

Now, let us suppose that exactly one hour after predicted high noon you measure the sun's height and find it to be 74° 32'. This is too high. You must continue shooting until the sun's height matches your morning shot. Four minutes later, at 14:22, you measure 74° 00'.

The time difference between your morning shot and your afternoon shot is 124 minutes. High noon occurred half way between these two shots, or 62 minutes after the first shot. Therefore, actual noon must have occurred at 12:18 + 62 minutes, or 13:20. This is two minutes after predicted noon.

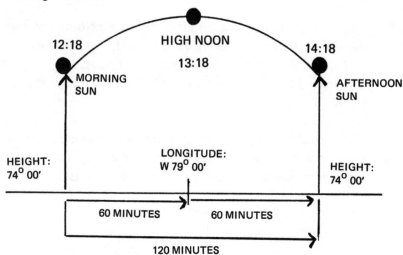

SITUATION: You are on your assumed longitude. Shooting the sun before and after high noon simply confirms this fact. Your predicted and measured high noon times are identical.

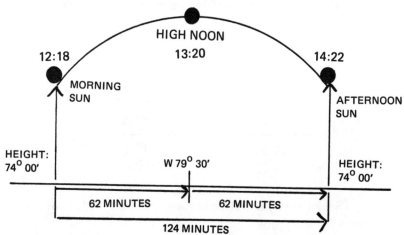

SITUATION: You are 30' west of your assumed longitude: W 79° 00'. Calculation of actual noon shows that it occurred two mintues later than predicted.

The earth turns at a rate of 15' of longitude for every minute of time. As you move westward, noon occurs later and later. Since actual noon was two minutes late, you are 2 X 15' = 30', or 30' west of W 79° 00'. Your noon longitude is: W 79° 30'.

Let us formalize this procedure. Start making a series of shots one hour before noon. Record the time and sextant readings minute by minute for about five minutes.

TIME	SEXTANT
12:16	73° 44'
12:17	73° 52'
12:18	74° 00'
12:19	74° 08'
12:20	74° 16'

About 50 minutes after the noon shot, begin another series of shots. You read:

TIME	SEXTANT
14:18	74° 16'
14:19	74° 08'
14:20	74° 00'
14:21	73° 52'
14:22	73° 44'

Select one pair of values and proceed with your calculation for longitude. (See next page.)

A SIMPLE LATITUDE CHECK

90° 00'	=	89° 60'
OBSERVED HEIGHT	=	81° 10' (SUBTRACT)
DISTANCE FROM TOWER	=	8° 50'
SUN'S DECLINATION	=	23° 26' (ADD IN SUMMER) (SUBTRACT IN WINTER)

YOUR LATITUDE IS: N 31° 76' = N 32° 16'

A SIMPLE LONGITUDE CHECK

MORNING SEXTANT: 74° 00' TIME: 12:18

AFTERNOON SEXTANT: 74° 00' TIME: 14:20

DIFFERENCE: 122 Minutes

DIFFERENCE DIVIDED BY TWO: 61 minutes

ACTUAL HIGH NOON: 13:19

LONGITUDE: W 79°   PREDICTED NOON: 13:18

ACTUAL NOON WAS: EARLY (LATE) : 1 (Minutes of Time)

X 15

PLUS IF LATE / MINUS IF EARLY: +15' (Minutes of Longitude)

Predicted Longitude: PLUS FOR WEST / MINUS FOR EAST + 79° (Degrees of Longitude)

YOUR LONGITUDE IS: W 79° 15' (TOTAL)

PRACTICE PROBLEM

You are now prepared to check your longitude during your trek to Bermuda. Using the morning and afternoon shots for June 21, calculate the time of actual noon, and your noon longitude for this day on your voyage to Bermuda.

DATE	SEXTANT	GMT	EDT
MORNING	71° 18'	16:04	12:04
JUNE 17	76° 30'		NOON
AFTERNOON	71° 18'	18:04	14:04
MORNING	72° 16'	15:57	11:57
JUNE 18	78° 00'		NOON
AFTERNOON	72° 16'	17:57	13:57
MORNING	73° 10'	15:50	11:50
JUNE 19	79° 30'		NOON
AFTERNOON	73° 10'	17:50	13:50
MORNING	74° 00'	15:42	11:42
JUNE 20	81° 00'		NOON
AFTERNOON	74° 00'	17:42	13:42
MORNING	74° 00'	15:32	11:32
JUNE 21	81° 08'		NOON
AFTERNOON	74° 00'	17:32	13:32
MORNING	74° 00'	15:24	11:24
JUNE 22	81° 10'		NOON
AFTERNOON	74° 00'	17:24	13:24

(Answers on page 123)

A SIMPLE LATITUDE CHECK

90⁰ 00'   =   89⁰ 60'

OBSERVED HEIGHT   =   (SUBTRACT)

_____

DISTANCE FROM TOWER   =

SUN'S DECLINATION   =   (ADD IN SUMMER)
                                            (SUBTRACT IN WINTER)

_____

YOUR LATITUDE IS :

_____

A SIMPLE LONGITUDE CHECK

MORNING SEXTANT :_____   TIME : _____

AFTERNOON SEXTANT :_____   TIME : _____

DIFFERENCE : _____

DIFFERENCE DIVIDED BY TWO : _____

ACTUAL HIGH NOON : _____

LONGITUDE : _____ PREDICTED NOON : _____

ACTUAL NOON WAS :   EARLY :   (Minutes
                                   LATE   _____ of Time)

                                                  X 15

                        PLUS IF LATE   (Minutes of
                        MINUS IF EARLY   _____ Longitude)

Predicted Longitude: PLUS FOR WEST   (Degrees of
                        MINUS FOR EAST   _____ Longitude)

_____

YOUR LONGITUDE IS: (TOTAL)

_____

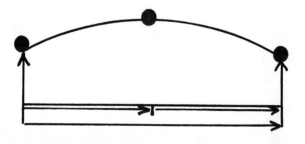

SUMMARY

You have now completed the emergency part of celestial navigation. You have two methods for calculating your latitude, and one method for obtaining your longitude. The simple longitude check will give you absolute confidence that Bermuda is *ahead of you* rather than behind you.

The next chapter will allow you to check your longitude any time in the afternoon. In fact, the procedure is basic for an understanding of the remaining part of celestial navigation. You may learn this more complex technique at your leisure, as *you have now nailed down your position.*

You should set this book aside and practice shooting the sun. If you are on land, find open water to the south of you and shoot the sun from the beach. If you are a weekend sailor, take your sextant with you and practice shooting from the deck of your ship. You should spend two hours shooting the sun before continuing with the next chapter.

CHAPTER III

THE LONGITUDE SHOT

Stop now and review what you have accomplished. When you started reading this book you did not know your position to within 1,000 miles. You had no experience with celestial navigation. For three hours of reading and practice with a sextant you:

1. Have found your latitude.
2. Have found your longitude.
3. Are developing skill with a sextant.
4. Are gaining familiarity with the Nautical Almanac.

The following method will require more diligence. If you have difficulty with *The Longitude Shot,* you may fall back on the techniques presented in the preceding chapters. It is hard for an intelligent man to follow an arbitrary procedure. Nevertheless, this is what this chapter requires. As the days go by, and you reduce more and more shots, you will see the reason and logic behind the procedure you are using. *You learn by doing.*

If you wish to visualize the positioning of your Ho Line of Position on your map, read the graphical technique presented in the next chapter.

Initially, to minimize your mental gymnastics, I suggest two temporary intellectual restrictions in this chapter. (Sail east or west, shoot the sun in the afternoon.) These will be easily removed in the next chapter. A triple check technique is presented in the next chapter which will allow you to detect any errors you might make.

Now that you know your latitude by the noon shot, you can begin work on the more complex longitude shot. The calculations have been simplified by using only the sun. The sun is used almost exclusively for celestial navigation by the small boat navigator.

This is the part of celestial navigation that requires time to learn. It normally takes about 50 hours to learn the theory and practice, which is why it has been so foreboding. You can shoot the sun *now* and reduce your shot *this afternoon.*

I have broken the form into small problems that are easily solved. The hardest shot to reduce is the first one. Each succeeding shot will further familiarize you with the work form.

In the next chapter I will show you that celestial navigation is nothing more than the measurement of exact distances across the surface of the earth.

HOW DO I MAKE MY SHOT?

The technique for the operation of the sextant is the same as for the noon shot; however, you must now record the exact time that you measure the sun's height. The procedure is to adjust the sextant until you have the sun exactly on the horizon, and then mark your time.

After you have obtained a sextant measurement with the exact time, you are ready to begin the sight reduction. This will give you a line of position which will cross your noon latitude and pinpoint your position. For purposes of this problem, you will sail due east between the noon shot and the longitude shot. It will simplify the plotting procedure.

HOW DO I OBTAIN THE SUN'S CALCULATED HEIGHT?

It is easy to become confused with the longitude shot. To avoid this you must keep in mind the fact that you are establishing three points on the surface of the earth. They are:

1. The North Pole.
2. The sun's position   (Base of the Sun's Tower.)
3. Your adjusted, or *assumed* position.

These three points form a triangle on the surface of the earth. The top of the triangle is the North Pole. The sides of the triangle are the longitude of the sun and the longitude of your assumed position. The angle between the two longitudes is called the *Local Hour Angle.*

THE NAVIGATION TRIANGLE
PRODUCED BY THE AFTERNOON SUN

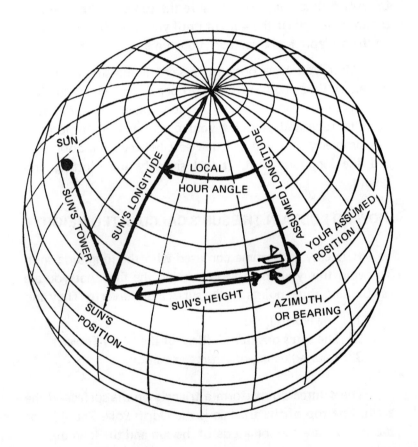

THE NAVIGATION TRIANGLE IS SOLVED BY "LOOK-UP" TABLES

Every time you work a problem in celestial navigation you are establishing this triangle and solving it for:

1. The sun's exact height.
2. The sun's bearing. (Also called azimuth.)

The work form supplied with the text is designed to help you pinpoint:

1. The sun's position.
2. The Local Hour Angle. (LHA)
3. Your assumed position.

Once you have established these three parts of the triangle you will "look-up" the sun's exact height and bearing.

Now, work out a complete shot. The work form is numbered to allow you to refer to the descriptive paragraphs.

HOW DO I REDUCE MY LONGITUDE SHOT?

(1) At a GMT of 19 hours and 20 minutes you obtain a sextant reading of 62° 02'. This is entered in the work form with the date and your estimated longitude. Your latitude, by the noon shot is N 32° 16'. Since you are sailing due east, your actual latitude is unchanged. (Page 51)

(2) Next, you "correct" your sextant reading. Your height-of-eye is nine feet. The sextant's index error is 13', "on arc". The semi-diameter and refraction value is 16'.

HOW DO I CALCULATE THE SUN'S GREENWICH HOUR ANGLE?

(3)   Your next task is to find the sun's position, as listed in the Nautical Almanac. The sun's declination (Dec.) is N 23° 26'. The Greenwich Hour Angle (GHA) is listed next to the declination and has the value of 104°31' for 19:00 hours.

This would be the sun's position if you made the shot on the hour. Since you made the shot 20 minutes after the hour, you must include the additional angle the earth turns in this time. The table is listed on the yellow pages and it is called "Increments and Corrections". The earth turns 5 degrees in 20 minutes. (See next page.) In the work form you add the 5 degrees to 104°31' which equals 109°31'. This is the sun's exact position at the instant you made your shot. This establishes *one point* of the triangle.

Let us graphically portray the location of the sun's tower in terms of latitude and longitude. The latitude is equivalent to the sun's declination, and the longitude is equivalent to the sun's Greenwich Hour Angle.

WHAT RULES DO I FOLLOW TO ASSUME A POSITION?

(4)   In order to calculate the sun's height and bearing you must assume a position. You must round off your latitude to the nearest whole number.

0° LONGITUDE

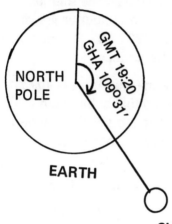

NORTH POLE

GMT 19:20
GHA 109° 31′

EARTH

SUN

JUNE 22, 1987

THE DAILY PAGE

22	00	179 33.9	N23	26.6
	01	194 33.8		26.6
	02	209 33.6		26.6
	03	224 33.5	..	26.6
	04	239 33.4		26.6
	05	254 33.2		26.6
	06	269 33.1	N23	26.6
	07	284 32.9		26.6
	08	299 32.8		26.5
M	09	314 32.7	..	26.5
O	10	329 32.5		26.5
N	11	344 32.4		26.5
D	12	359 32.3	N23	26.5
A	13	14 32.1		26.5
Y	14	29 32.0		26.5
	15	44 31.9	..	26.5
	16	59 31.7		26.5
	17	74 31.6		26.5
	18	89 31.4	N23	26.4
	19	104 31.3		26.4
	20	119 31.2		26.4

HOUR	19:	= 104°31′
MINUTE	:20	= 5°00′ (add)
GMT	19:20	= 109°31′ GHA

THE YELLOW PAGES:

20ᵐ	SUN PLANETS
s	° ′
00	5 00·0
01	5 00·3
02	5 00·5
03	5 00·8
04	5 01·0

THE SUN'S POSITION

Sun's Longitude: 109°31′
Sun's Greenwich Hour Angle: 109°31′

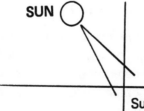

SUN

Sun's Latitude: N 23° 26′

Sun's Declination: N 23° 26′

You *must* assume a position to allow the use of a "look-up" table. These tables are made up in two books called HO 249; Volumes 2 and 3. They contain the solution for your triangle for all integer latitudes, local hour angles, and declinations. Your noon latitude is 32° 16'. Round this off to N 32° 00'. This is your *assumed* latitude.

Since the sun's Greenwich Hour Angle is 109°31' you must "round" your longitude so that subtraction will result in an integer number. By adjusting your longitude to 79° 31' you cause the required subtraction to result in an integer local hour angle.

Greenwich Hour Angle	109° 31'
Assumed Longitude W	79° 31' (Subtract if west)
Local Hour Angle	30° 00'

Footnotes #1 and #3 (Do I add 360°? Do I subtract 360°?) do not apply to this problem; they will be explained in the next chapter. Footnote #2 states: Subtract the longitude *if it is west.* Since you are on a west longitude you subtract your longitude from the Greenwich Hour Angle.

⑤   In the work form, under *ASSUMED POSITION* enter:

N 32° 00' and W 79° 31'

This is the *second point* of the triangle.

HOW DO I LOOK UP THE SUN'S HEIGHT AND BEARING?

HO 249 has the solution for all triangles that can be formed using integer values. You are ready to use Volume 2 (latitudes 0° to 40°) to determine the sun's height and bearing. In the work form enter the Local Hour Angle, the sun's declination and your latitude.

YOUR ASSUMED POSITION

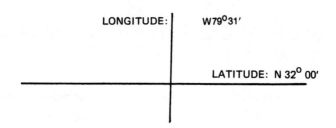

LONGITUDE: | W79°31'

LATITUDE: N 32° 00'

RULES FOR SELECTING YOUR ASSUMED POSITION

1. You *must* "round" your latitude off to the nearest whole number of degrees.

2. You *must* "round" your longitude to get a whole number of degrees for your local hour angle.

THE LOCAL HOUR IS AN INTEGER NUMBER

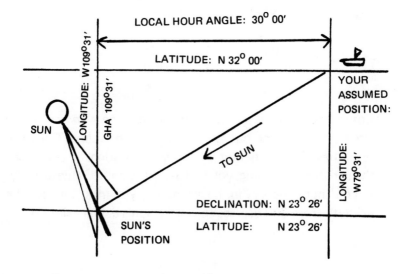

LOCAL HOUR ANGLE: 30° 00'

LONGITUDE: W109°31'

GHA 109°31'

LATITUDE: N 32° 00'

YOUR ASSUMED POSITION:

LONGITUDE: W79°31'

SUN

TO SUN

DECLINATION: N 23° 26'

SUN'S POSITION

LATITUDE: N 23° 26'

⑥ LHA   SUN'S DEC.   LATITUDE (ASSUMED)

30°00' N *23°26'* (Same) N *32°00'*
LOCAL HOUR ANGLE   Contrary

HO 249 is made up of pages for whole latitudes, labeled "SAME" and "CONTRARY". If your latitude and declination are both North, or both South, you circle "SAME". If they are different, you circle "CONTRARY". Since both the latitude and declination are north, you circle "SAME". (See above.)

Searching through HO 249, you find several pages for latitude 32 degrees. Further looking through these pages produces a page called "SAME NAME", and declinations from 15° to 29°. You are now prepared to find your calculated height and bearing of the sun. (Next page)

For a local hour angle of 30 degrees and a declination of 23 degrees, you obtain the following:

⑦   62° 01'   +25   101
          Hc   d   Z

Enter these values in the work form *where indicated by circles.* First, work out the Z, or azimuth value. The form simplifies the calculation of the sun's bearing. If you shoot the sun in the morning, you will use the azimuth value directly. If you shoot the sun in the afternoon, you must subtract the azimuth from 360 degrees to get the sun's actual azimuth.

SUN

(2) Sextant Observations

Sextant: _62° 02'_
I.E. _− 13'_
Height-of-Eye _− 03'_
SD & Refraction _+ 16'_

Total: Ho = _62° 02'_

(1) Deduced Position

Date _JUNE 22, 1987_ _N 32° 16'_ Latitude
Day _Monday_
GMT _19:20:00_
Corr? _:00_ _W 79° 15'_ Longitude
GMT _19:20:00_

(3) **SUN'S POSITION – From the Nautical Almanac**

Dec. _N 23° 26'_ GMT
Hour _19:_   GHA _104° 31'_
Minutes, Seconds _20:00_   (+) _5° 00'_
Dec. _N 23° 26'_ GMT: _19:20:00_   GHA: _109° 31'_
(+ 360)   1.

(4) Local Hour Angle = GHA +/− Longitude

Greenwich Hour Angle . . . . GHA: _109° 31'_
Assumed Longitude . . . . _79° 31'_ 2.
TOTAL: Local Hour Angle _30° 00'_
(− 360)   3.
Local Hour Angle . . . . _30° 00'_

(5) Assumed Position: Latitude _32° 00'_   Longitude _W 79° 31'_

(6) Find the Sun's Height and Bearing Using HO 249

Sun's Declination   Latitude (Assumed)

_30° 00'_   N _23° 26'_ Same Contrary N _32° 00'_
Local Hour Angle

(7) Sun's Hc Interpolation Table   Sun's Bearing   4.
Dec. _23°_   Hc _62° 01'_   360

d _+ 25_ × _26_ /60= _+ 11_   Z = _101°_   Morning Azimuth

Dec. _N 23° 26'_ Hc _62° 12'_   _259°_   Afternoon Azimuth

Ho & Hc   Hc = _62° 12'_
Comparison   Ho = _62° 02'_

_10'_   Towards / Away (Difference)

(8) HoMoTo

ADJUST

N 32

FROM HO 249

DECLINATION (15°-29°) SAME NAME AS LATITUDE

LHA	15° Hc	d	Z	16° Hc	d	Z	22° Hc	d	Z	23° Hc	d	Z	24° Hc	d	Z
	° ′	′	°	° ′	′	°	° ′	′	°	° ′	′	°	° ′	′	°
0	73 00	+60	180	74 00	+60	180	80 00	+60	180	81 00	+60	180	82 00	+60	180
1	72 59	60	177	73 59	59	177	79 58	59	175	80 57	60	174	81 57	60	174
2	72 54	60	173	73 54	60	173	79 51	59	169	80 50	59	168	81 49	58	167
3	72 47	59	170	73 46	59	170	79 39	58	164	80 37	57	163	81 34	57	161
4	72 37	59	167	73 36	58	166	79 23	57	159	80 20	55	158	81 15	55	155
25	61 35	+39	121	62 14	+38	119	65 40	+29	108	66 09	+26	106	66 35	+25	104
26	60 51	39	120	61 30	37	118	64 51	28	107	65 19	27	105	65 46	24	103
27	60 07	37	118	60 44	37	117	64 03	27	106	64 30	26	104	64 56	24	102
28	59 22	37	117	59 59	36	116	63 13	28	105	63 41	25	103	64 06	24	101
29	58 36	37	116	59 13	35	114	62 24	27	104	62 51	25	102	63 16	24	100
30	57 50	+36	115	58 26	+35	113	61 35	+26	103	62 01	+25	101	62 26	+23	99
31	57 04	35	114	57 39	34	112	60 45	26	102	61 11	25	100	61 36	23	99
32	56 17	35	113	56 52	34	111	59 55	26	101	60 21	24	100	60 45	23	98
33	55 30	34	112	56 04	34	110	59 05	26	101	59 31	24	99	59 55	22	97
34	54 43	34	111	55 17	32	109	58 15	26	100	58 41	23	98	59 04	23	96

TABLE 5. — Correction to Tabulated Altitude for Minutes of Declination

d / ′	1	2	3	4	5	6	7	8	9	22	23	24	25	26	27	28	29	30
0	0	0	0	0	0	0	0	0	0	0	0	0	0	0	0	0	0	0
1	0	0	0	0	0	0	0	0	0	0	0	0	0	0	0	0	0	0
2	0	0	0	0	0	0	0	0	0	1	1	1	1	1	1	1	1	1
3	0	0	0	0	0	0	0	0	0	1	1	1	1	1	1	1	1	2
4	0	0	0	0	0	0	0	1	1	1	2	2	2	2	2	2	2	2
20	0	1	1	1	2	2	2	3	3	7	8	8	8	9	9	9	10	10
21	0	1	1	1	2	2	2	3	3	8	8	8	9	9	9	10	10	10
22	0	1	1	1	2	2	3	3	3	8	8	9	9	10	10	10	11	11
23	0	1	1	2	2	2	3	3	3	8	9	9	10	10	10	11	11	12
24	0	1	1	2	2	2	3	3	4	9	10	10	10	10	11	11	12	12
25	0	1	1	2	2	2	3	3	4	9	10	10	10	11	11	12	12	12
26	0	1	1	2	2	3	3	3	4	10	10	10	11	11	12	12	13	13
27	0	1	1	2	2	3	3	4	4	10	10	11	11	12	12	13	13	14
28	0	1	1	2	2	3	3	4	4	10	11	11	12	12	13	13	14	14
29	0	1	1	2	2	3	3	4	4	11	11	12	12	13	13	14	14	14

SUN'S BEARING

$$Z = \begin{array}{l} 360^\circ \\ \underline{101 \quad \text{MORNING AZIMUTH}} \\ 259 \quad \text{AFTERNOON AZIMUTH} \end{array}$$

Your Z value was 101 degrees. This would be the sun's bearing if you shot the sun in the morning. You made the shot in the afternoon. Subtract 101° from 360°. The result, 259°, is the sun's bearing at the time you made your shot. (If you are south of the equator you must use the azimuth calculation table on the pictorial page of the work form.) (Page 64, Footnote No. 4.)

HOW DO I "ADJUST" THE SUN'S HEIGHT FOR MINUTES OF DECLINATION?

HO 249 gives you the height of the sun for a declination of 23° 00′. You must interpolate to find the height of the sun for a declination of 23° 26′. The sun's Hc INTER-POLATION TABLE is designed to help you account for minutes of declination.

SUN'S Hc INTERPOLATION TABLE

| Declination: | 23° | = Height of: 62° 01′ |
| d = + 25 | 26′ = | + 11′ |

Declination: 23° 26′ = Height of: 62° 12′

One procedure is to multiply + 25 X 26′ / 60. The result, 11′, is then added to the Hc of the sun. (The result will be added if the d value is positive, and subtracted if the d value is negative.)

An easier way to accomplish this calculation is to use a table to do the required multiplication and division. (Previous page). This table is found on the last page of HO 249. At the top of the page you find the d value; on the left you find the (') value. Where row and column intersect you find a value of + 11. Enter 11' in the interpolation table and complete the calculation as shown above. For a declination of N 23° 26', the sun's height is 62° 12'.

HOW DO I SKETCH MY TRIANGLE ON THE EARTH'S SURFACE?

The work form can be confusing. To keep a clear picture of what you are doing, it is essential that you sketch and label the triangle you are forming. You have calculated the sun's height and bearing, which is 62° 12' at a bearing of 259°. This is the exact height of the sun at position: N 32° 00' and W 79° 31'. This completes the solution of the triangle you have created. Sketch and label your triangle for:

1. The sun's position: N 23° 26' & W 109° 31'
2. Your position: N 32° 00' & W 79° 31'
3. Your Local Hour Angle: 30° 00'

You have solved this triangle for:

1. The sun's exact height: 62° 12'
2. The sun's bearing: 259°

After you establish your triangle you look up
the sun's height and bearing:
Calculated height = 62° 12'
Azimuth = 259°

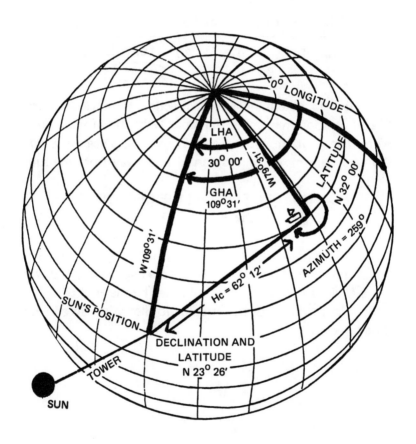

HOW DO I COMPARE MY OBSERVED HEIGHT
WITH MY CALCULATED HEIGHT?

(8) Well, that's a lot of work . . . but the hard part is done. The fun part is plotting your resulting lines of position. But first, you must compare your calculated height with your observed height. The difference is 10' of angle.

Hc Calculated Height	62° 12'	
Ho Observed Height	62° 02'	

Ho Mo To	10'	Towards	(Difference)
		~~Away~~	

To help determine which direction to move your Ho line of position, remember the word HoMoTo. If your *Ho* is *Mo*re than your Hc, move *To*wards the sun. Since this *is not* the case, you move your observed line away from the sun.

HOW DO I PLOT MY Ho LINE OF POSITION
ON MY MAP?

To determine your longitude you must plot your Ho line of position on your map. If you are mid-ocean, you will use a *Universal Plotting Chart* published by the Hydrographic Office. You will need a protractor to plot your Ho and Hc lines of position.

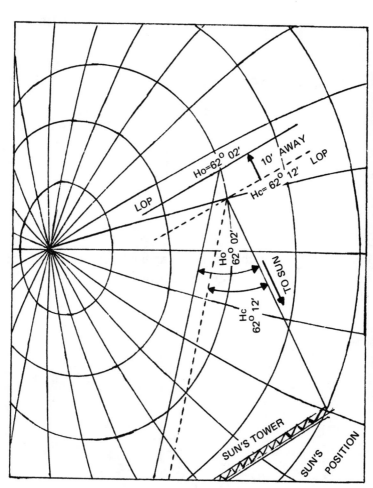

STEP #1

Mark or label your chart with your *assumed* latitude and longitude.

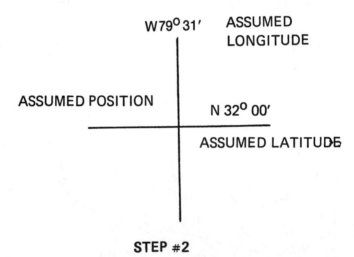

STEP #2

The second step is to plot a dotted line on a bearing of 259 degrees through your assumed position. Label this line "TO SUN".

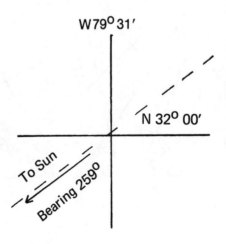

STEP #3

The third step is to plot a dotted line at right angles to the first dotted line — through your assumed position. Label the second line: Hc = 62° 12'

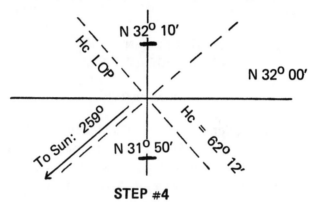

STEP #4

The fourth step is to measure 10' "away" along the sun's dotted line. Plot your Ho Line of Position 10' away from the sun and away from your Hc Line of Position. Use your dividers to lay off 10' (10 nautical miles) from the Hc Line of Position. Label the Line: Ho = 62° 02'. You have now plotted all the information contained in the afternoon shot.

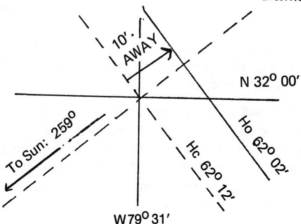

Since you have been sailing east along a latitude of N 32° 16', you must still be on this latitude. Draw a horizontal line along N 32° 16' and label it "Noon Latitude". The point where the noon latitude intersects your afternoon Ho line of position pinpoints your present location. A plot of this will give you:

LATITUDE: N 32° 16'
LONGITUDE: W 79° 22'

SUMMARY

Congratulations! You have just completed *One Day Celestial Navigation — At Sea.* This afternoon you will have (for three hours of study) found your longitude. This is the hard part of celestial navigation. During the following days you will:

1. Shoot the sun at noon to get your latitude.
2. Shoot the sun two (2) hours later to get your longitude.

Every shot you make will further increase your skill in celestial navigation. You will develop familiarity with the work form, the Nautical Almanac, and HO 249, which is essential for competent navigation. By advancing your noon latitude (next chapter) you may sail in any direction and shoot the sun at any time. Learning to advance your noon line of position takes about 30 minutes.

You will find that each afternoon shot is similar to the previous shot. After six sight reductions you will be sufficiently skilled to begin to use the special techniques presented in the next chapter. After you have gained some experience, you will find that it takes about 10 minutes to reduce the longitude shot.

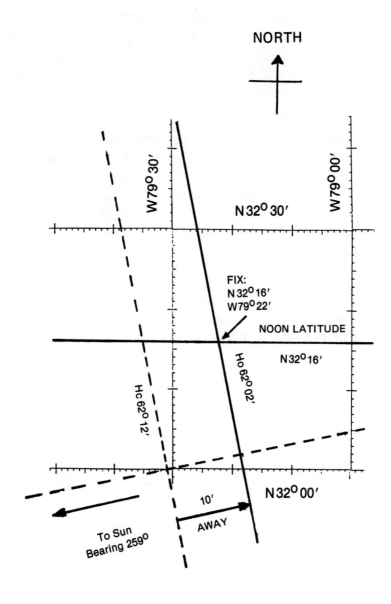

HOW DO I USE A UNIVERSAL PLOTTING SHEET?

If you are mid-ocean, you may use the *Universal Plotting Sheet.* You will duplicate the previous plotting method. Your fix is established by the intersection of your noon line of position and your afternoon line of position.

The universal chart does not have lines of longitude printed on it. To measure the longitude "compression" it is necessary to use the smaller "mid-latitude" graph printed on the lower right-hand side of the chart. Draw a horizontal line on the mid-latitude graph at 32°. On the main chart, set your dividers for the distance between the center line (assumed longitude) and your fix. Going to the smaller graph, you read this distance as 9' of longitude.

Your longitude is 9' east of your assumed longitude. Your actual longitude is $W79^O31' - 9' = W79^O22'$. *YOUR POSITION IS:* $N32^O16'$ & $W79^O22'$.

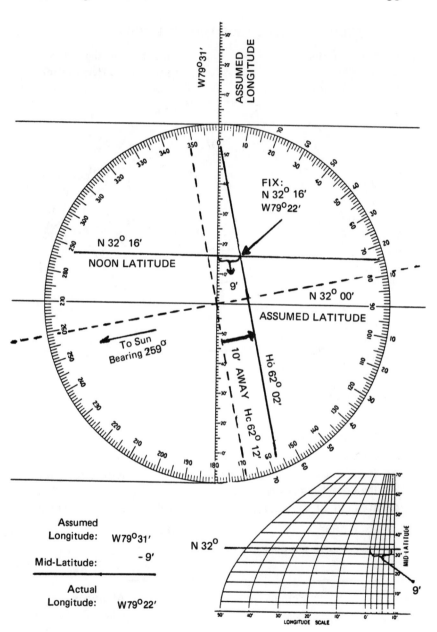

W79°31'

ASSUMED
LONGITUDE

FIX:
N 32° 16'
W79°22'

N 32° 16'
NOON LATITUDE

9'

N 32° 00'
ASSUMED LATITUDE

To Sun
Bearing 259°

10' AWAY   Hc 62° 12'

Hó 62° 02'

Assumed	
Longitude:	W79°31'
Mid-Latitude:	- 9'
Actual	
Longitude:	W79°22'

N 32°

MID-LATITUDE

9'

LONGITUDE SCALE

SKETCH AND LABEL YOUR TRIANGLE FOR:

I	Sun's Position.	IV	Greenwich Hour Angle.
II	Your Position.	V	Sun's Calculated Height. (Hc)
III	Local Hour Angle.	VI	Sun's Bearing.

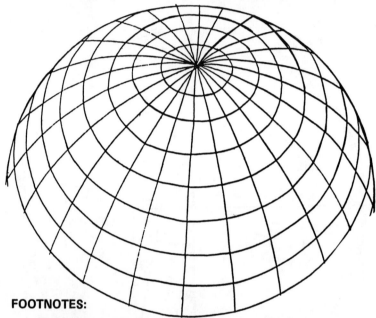

FOOTNOTES:

1. If subtracting your west longitude results in a negative number, add 360° to the Greenwich Hour Angle.

2. Subtract the longitude if West. Add Longitude if east.

3. If the Local Hour Angle is greater than 360°, subtract 360° from the Local Hour Angle.

4. If south of the equator, use the following bearing calculations:

	180°		180°
Z =	Subtract	Z =	Add
	———		———
	Morning Bearing		Afternoon Bearing

SUN

2   Sextant Observations   **1**   Deduced Position

Sextant: _____   Date _____
                                                              Latitude
I.E. _____   Day _____

Height-of-Eye _____   GMT _____

SD & Refraction_____   Corr? _____
                                                              Longitude
Total: Ho =   GMT _____

3   **SUN'S POSITION – From the Nautical Almanac**

Dec. _____   GMT
                        Hour _____   GHA _____

          Minutes, Seconds_____   (+) _____

Dec.   GMT: GHA:
                                              (+ 360)   **1.**

4   Local Hour Angle = GHA +/ – Longitude

Greenwich Hour Angle . . . . GHA: _____

Assumed Longitude . . . . _____ **2.**

          TOTAL: Local Hour Angle_____

                                              (–360)   **3.**

Local Hour Angle . . . .

ADJUST

5 Assumed Position: Latitude   Longitude

6   Find the Sun's Height and Bearing Using HO 249

               Sun's Declination   Latitude (Assumed)

                              Same
_____ _____ Contrary _____ _____
Local Hour Angle

7   Sun's Hc Interpolation Table   Sun's Bearing   **4.**
Dec. _____   Hc _____   360

                                              Z = _____   Morning
d _____ X ___ /60= _____ _____   Azimuth
                                                            Afternoon
Dec. _____   Hc _____   Azimuth

Ho & Hc
Comparison
               _____
                              Towards
8   HoMoTo   Away   (Difference)

PRACTICE PROBLEM

On your voyage to Bermuda you shot the sun on the afternoon of June 21, this year. You obtain a sextant reading of *74⁰ 00′ at a GMT 17:32.* Your noon latitude was N 32⁰ 18′. Your estimated longitude was W 67⁰ 30′. You are sailing on a true heading of 90 degrees — due east. *What is your latitude and longitude* at the time you made your afternoon shot?

COMPREHENSIVE REVIEW

It is a high point in your navigation career when you can put your finger on two crossed lines on your map and say, "This is where I am". These three chapters give you that capability. Working practice problems is boring. Working your own shot, while at sea, is a challenge. The technique given in this section is what celestial navigation is all about. If you can persevere through this chapter — shooting the sun and marking your time, finding the sun's position in the Nautical Almanac, solving the triangle using HO 249, and finally plotting your Ho line of position on your map — you have made it!

It is now up to *you* to carry through with actual shots of the sun. You should not continue with the next chapter until you have shot the sun *at sea* a number of times. Essentially, this chapter completes *ONE DAY CELESTIAL NAVIGATION.* The next chapter is icing on the cake.

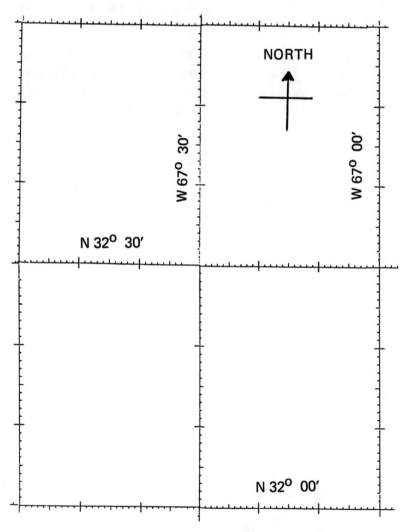

PLOT YOUR POSITION

You can now understand why the calculated height procedure was presented first. It is an exact duplicate of the longitude procedure used in this chapter. If you understand the Ho – Hc practices to start with, you will have no problem with them when encountered in this section.

The "final exam" is not a test I can give you. When you see the green of an island materialize on the blue horizon, after several days at sea . . . this is the ultimate test of your ability. It is quite a thrill when you do it for the first time.

CHAPTER IV

SPECIAL TECHNIQUES

You are now pinpointing your position by plotting crossed lines of position on your map. Shooting and plotting the sun in the morning is identical to the afternoon shot . . . except for the Local Hour Angle procedure. This section will help you remove the two initial restrictions. (Sail east or west, shoot the sun in the afternoon.) Advancing your noon Line of Position is the simplest part of celestial navigation.

HOW DO I ADVANCE MY NOON LINE OF POSITION?

When you sail east or west, your noon line of position and advanced Line of Position are identical. (N 32° 16') The distance you have moved along your noon line need not be considered. Obviously, you cannot always sail east or west between the noon shot and the afternoon shot.

Let's assume you're sailing north for two hours after the noon shot at a speed of 5 knots. Your distance run between the noon shot and the afternoon shot is:

2 hours X 5 knots = 10 nautical miles

Since you sailed due north, you advance your noon latitude by 10 nautical miles. At GMT 19:20, you are on:

N 32° 16' + 10' = Latitude N 32° 26'

At the time of the afternoon shot you were on latitude N 32° 26'. When you reduce your afternoon shot, the afternoon Line of Position will cross N 32° 26' and fix your position.

What about the intermediate case, where you sail at some other heading — — say 60°? In this situation you will lay off 10' on a bearing of 60 degrees. This will advance your noon latitude to N 32° 21'. Again, your afternoon LOP will cross this latitude and fix your position.

Any line of position can be advanced by the use of DR information (Distance run in a known direction.) In actual practice, you can cross two lines made three hours apart. On a cloudy day it is possible to get only two glimpses of the sun — separated by several hours — and yet fix your position. (The process of advancing your first Line of Position to cross it with the second Line of Position is called a running fix.)

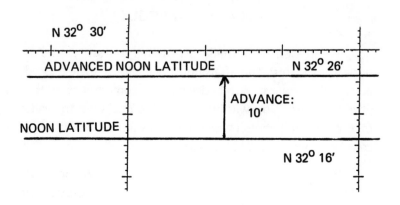

SITUATION: You have sailed due north after your noon shot. You are 10 miles north of latitude N 32° 16'.

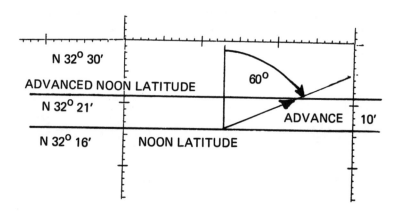

SITUATION: You sail 10 miles on a bearing of 60°. This puts you on a latitude N 32° 21.

HOW DO I CALCULATE A MORNING
LOCAL HOUR ANGLE?

The reason for initially restricting yourself to the afternoon shot is this: The afternoon Local Hour Angle procedure is straightforward. After developing competence with the afternoon shot you will be prepared to deal with the vagaries of the morning shot. These difficulties are caused by the procedural way the Local Hour Angle is handled.

You shall be required to adjust your GHA and LHA by adding or subtracting 360°. The rules for doing Local Hour Angle calculations follow this line of thought. They are designed to produce a LHA from 0° to 360°. (No negative numbers, and no LHA's greater than 360°.)

Your Local Hour Angle is *always* measured westward from your position. (See page 75) At noon the LHA is 0°, and as the earth turns increases by 15° per hour. At sunset the LHA is approximately 130° in summer, and at sunrise 230°. In the morning the LHA will increase from 230° to 360°. The footnotes must form a LHA that is within 0° to 360°.

FOOTNOTES

1. MUST I ADD 360° TO THE GREENWICH HOUR ANGLE?

Examine the Greenwich Hour Angle. Will subtraction of the west longitude produce a negative Local Hour Angle? If it will, you must add 360° to the Greenwich Hour Angle *before* subtracting your longitude. Example:

$$
\begin{array}{rl}
\text{GHA} & \quad 15°\ 22' \\
+ & 360°\ 00' \quad ? \\
\hline
& \quad 15°\ 22' \\
- & \quad 75°\ 22' \quad \text{Longitude (assumed)} \\
\hline
- & \quad 60°\ 00' \quad \text{A negative number —} \\
& \qquad\qquad\qquad\qquad \text{try again !}
\end{array}
$$

$$
\begin{array}{rl}
\text{GHA} & \quad 15°\ 22' \\
+ & 360°\ 00' \quad ? \\
\hline
& \ 375°\ 22' \\
- & \quad 75°\ 22' \quad \text{Longitude (assumed)} \\
\hline
& \ 300°\ 00' \quad \text{A morning Local Hour} \\
& \qquad\qquad\qquad\qquad \text{Angle}
\end{array}
$$

(The morning Local Hour Angles are listed on the right-hand side of the page in HO 249.)

2. DO I ADD OR SUBTRACT MY LONGITUDE?

If you are *west* of Greenwich, England (the prime meridian) you will subtract the West longitude from the Greenwich Hour Angle. If you are *east* of the prime meridian, you will add the East longitude to the Greenwich Hour Angle to obtain your Local Hour Angle.

If you are on an east longitude you must adjust your assumed longitude so the sum will be an integer Local Hour Angle.

GHA	$47^O\ 40'$	
E	$12^O\ 20'$	Longitude (assumed)
	$60^O\ 00'$	Local Hour Angle.

3.   MUST I SUBTRACT 360° FROM THE LOCAL HOUR ANGLE?

The result of the two preceding footnotes may occasionally produce a Local Hour Angle greater than 360°. If this occurs, simply subtract 360° from your Local Hour Angle to arrive at a LHA in the range of 0° to 360°.

GHA	$330^O\ 45'$
E	$89^O\ 15'$ Longitude (assumed)
	$420^O\ 00'$ (The LHA is greater than 360°.)
	$-\ 360^O\ 00'$?
	$60^O\ 00$

Since the earth turns at 15 degrees per hour, you can check your approximate Local Hour Angle by reference to the following table:

Morning Local Hour Angle	Hours Before or after noon	Afternoon Local Hour angle
360°	High Noon	0°
345°	1 Hour	15°
330°	2 Hours	30°
315°	3 Hours	45°
300°	4 Hours	60°
285°	5 Hours	75°
270°	6 Hours	90°
255°	7 Hours	105°
240°	8 Hours	120°

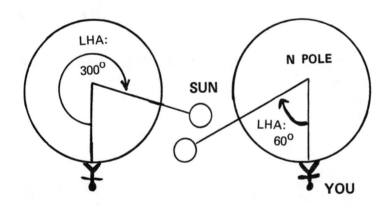

EARTH   EARTH

THE MORNING
LOCAL HOUR ANGLE

THE AFTERNOON
LOCAL HOUR ANGLE

FOUR HOURS BEFORE HIGH NOON   FOUR HOURS AFTER HIGH NOON

PRACTICE PROBLEM

Using the June 21st morning shot you made on your voyage to Bermuda, calculate and plot your morning position. * (Sextant: 74° 00', GMT: 15:32)

Always sketch your navigation triangle on the earth's surface; it will help you visualize the Local Hour Angle you are forming. The morning shot is identical to the afternoon shot — except for the Local Hour Angle.

This completes the major work of this book. Your standard procedure will be to:

    1. Shoot the sun; morning, noon and afternoon.
    2. Plot the three lines of position on your map.

These three shots will triangulate, triple checking your position.

There are two components of celestial navigation that this book cannot supply. One is the experience of using a sextant on a small boat. This can only be learned by doing it. The other is skill in reducing your shot. Only *your* interest and work can supply this necessary ingredient.

    * For the practice problems in this chapter use these sextant corrections: Index Error 13', on arc;   Height-of-eye 9 feet;   SD and refraction + 16'.

SOPHISTICATED TECHNIQUES

You are fully equipped to do a skilled job of navigating your vessel. We can introduce some art and sophistication into the basic technique. Very often, a single shot of the sun will be all you need for effective navigation.

If you are close to the base of the sun's tower, an easy plotting method makes position finding obvious and quick. Reviewing this method, as you shoot the sun, should help you more fully digest the concepts used in the longitude shot.

The computer has become prominent in navigation. Hand-held calculators can serve as a learning aid and as a back-up for HO 249. Any calculator having trigonometric functions (sin, cos, and tan) will serve; however, the "key stroke" programmable types are of more practical use.

We have not considered shots of the stars, moon and planets . . . for good reason. As a practical matter these objects are of little interest to the small boat navigator. For example, a professional navigator — Robin Knox Johnson — sailed non-stop around the world using *only* the sun for celestial navigation. This should tell you something about the usefulness of star navigation. Of academic interest, yes! Of practical use? Very limited for the small boat navigator.

IN WHICH DIRECTION IS MY ISLAND?

The main purpose of navigation is to answer your question: "If I continue my present heading, will I see my island?" One shot of the sun will answer your question. To obtain a *course* Line of Position, you must wait until the sun is 90° to your heading. (The sun is abeam.) This will cause the sun's Line of Position to lie directly on course.

You are northeast of Bermuda. You are not sure of your position, but are steering a southwest heading. You shoot the sun as it lies abeam.* When you plot the resulting Line of Position, you find that your heading of 232° will cause you to miss Bermuda by 20 nautical miles. (Next page)

You are *on* the Ho Line of Position, approximately 90 miles from Bermuda. Using this information you can see that you must turn about 12° to starboard to arrive at Bermuda.

THE MAGNETIC COMPASS

You may use the information obtained from the *on course* shot to point your boat at your island. Applying this information to your magnetic compass avoids consideration of magnetic variation or compass deviation (error).

* Sextant 78° 08'   GMT 15:40   GHA 55° 00'   DEC N 23° 26'

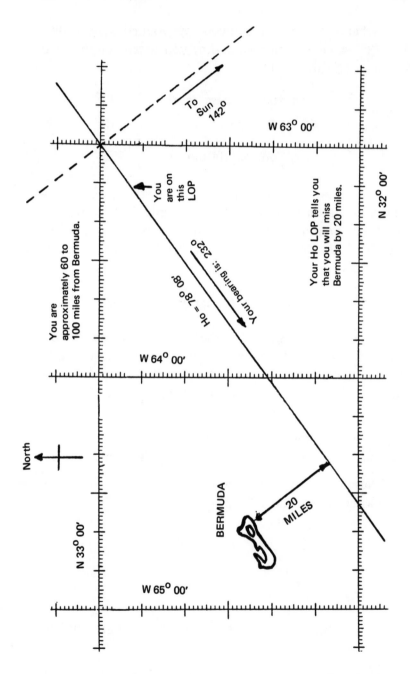

When you shoot the sun you note your compass reading as 243°. After reducing your shot you determine that you require a 12° turn to the right.

Magnetic Compass Reading	243°
12° Starboard	+ 12°
New Compass Heading	255°

Within several minutes — before or after your shot — trim your heading so your boat is exactly 90° to the sun; then read your magnetic compass. Assuming the compass read 243°, the new heading will be 255°, with a high degree of accuracy.

HOW FAR AM I FROM MY ISLAND?

Again, a single shot of the sun will tell you exactly how many miles there are between you and your island. Wait until the sun is dead ahead — or dead astern. When you shoot the sun, its height will provide an *exact mileage* scale of the distance between you and the island.

You shoot the sun when it is ahead*. You plot the sun's Line of Position and find that you are 76 miles from Bermuda.

Now, work the preceding two problems using HO 249. Your assumed position is N 33° 00′ & W 63° 00′.

* Sextant 71° 00′   GMT 18:16   GHA 82° 00   DEC N 23° 26′

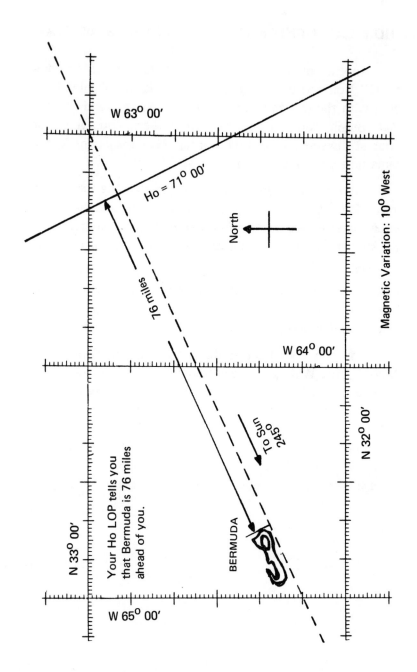

W 63° 00'

Ho = 71° 00'

North

Magnetic Variation: 10° West

76 miles

W 64° 00'

N 32° 00'

To Sun 245°

N 33° 00'

Your Ho LOP tells you that Bermuda is 76 miles ahead of you.

BERMUDA

W 65° 00'

HOW CAN I CHECK MY SHIP'S COMPASS AT SEA?

Another question is: "How accurate is my ship's compass?" You can check the ship's compass by aligning your boat with the setting or rising sun. Sailing westward towards Palm Beach, you observe the sun in the west. You point your boat at the sun and read its bearing: $280°$ magnetic. At the same time you shoot the sun.

After reducing your shot, you find that the sun's bearing is $280°$ true. The magnetic variation (as obtained from your chart) is zero degrees. Since your magnetic compass and the sun's bearing are both $280°$, *your compass has no error.*

What should you do if the variation is not zero? You may use the magnetic variation on your chart to convert true bearings to magnetic bearing. A magnetic and true compass rose is printed on your chart for this purpose. (Next page)

You aim your boat at the setting sun off Cape Sable, Nova Scotia. With your boat pointed at the sun, your compass reads $280°$ magnetic. From your sight reduction you obtain a true bearing of $260°$. The magnetic variation is $20°$ west. Adding $20°$ to $260°$ equals $280°$, which is the magnetic bearing of the sun. (If you draw a line on your compass rose, you will get the same result.) Since $260°$ true is the same as $280°$ magnetic, your compass has no error.

THE COMPASS ROSE IS USED TO ESTABLISH THE RELATION BETWEEN TRUE BEARINGS AND MAGNETIC BEARINGS

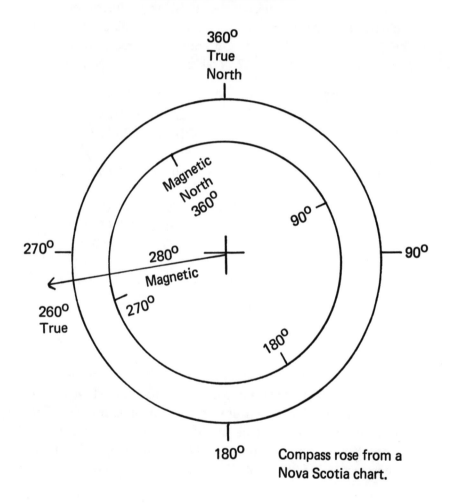

Compass rose from a
Nova Scotia chart.

HOW CAN I PINPOINT MY POSITION USING A GRAPHICAL TECHNIQUE?

If the sun passes within 420 miles, you can plot your Line of Position by placing the sun's tower directly on your chart. This is a simpler and more obvious technique than using HO 249. Sailing due east at 5 knots, you predict that noon will occur at GMT 17:02. You shoot the sun and obtain:

SEXTANT: 87° 00'   GMT: 17:02
GHA 75° 00'
DEC N 23° 26'

Twenty-four minutes later you again shoot the sun and obtain:

SEXTANT: 84° 00'   GMT: 17:26
GHA   81° 00'
DEC   N 23° 26'

You plot the sun's position directly on your chart. Your exact distance from the sun was:

$$90° - 87° = 3° \text{ AND } 90° - 84° = 6°$$

Using your compass, you draw a 3° circle around the base of the first tower and a 6° circle around the base of the second tower. Since you are on the Ho circle produced by both towers, you must be at the intersection of these two lines. You read your latitude and longitude directly from the chart as: N 26° 26' & W 75° 15'.

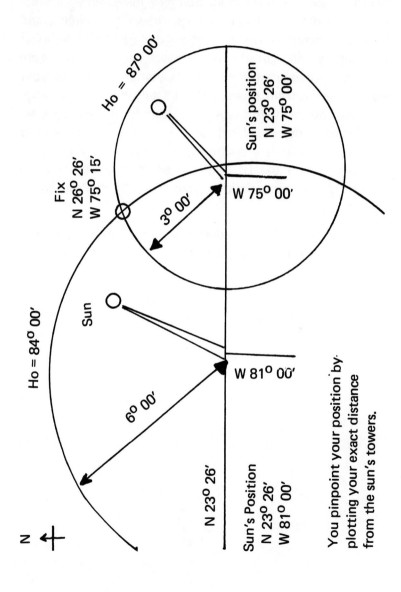

Ho = 87° 00'

Fix
N 26° 26'
W 75° 15'

Sun's position
N 23° 26'
W 75° 00'

W 75° 00'

3° 00'

Ho = 84° 00'

Sun

W 81° 00'

6° 00'

N 23° 26'

Sun's Position
N 23° 26'
W 81° 00'

N

You pinpoint your position by
plotting your exact distance
from the sun's towers.

The solution of this problem reveals the basic simplicity of celestial navigation. You have measured your exact distance from two known points, drawn two circles, and fixed your position. This type of celestial navigation is similar to sailing within sight of two light towers whose positions are known. By measuring their heights you are measuring your distance away from them. Unfortunately, the earth's curvature does not allow this type of solution for distances greater than 7 or 8 degrees. Much of the extra work of HO 249 occurs because it is a mathematical solution to a graphical problem. (Using the HO 249 procedure, you must erect a scaffold to properly position your Ho Line of Position on your map.)

Now, work the preceding graphical problem using HO 249. Your resulting position will be identical to the graphical solution.

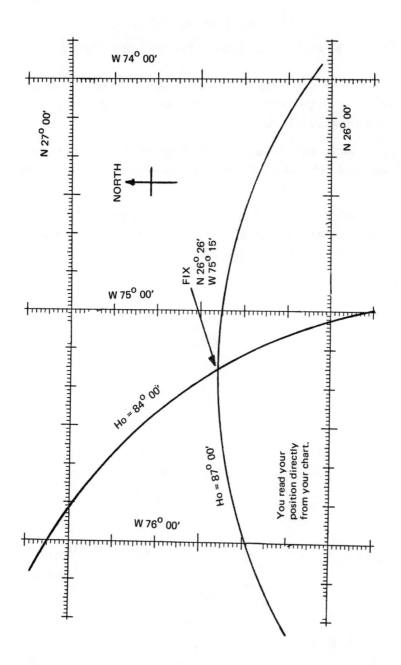

CALCULATOR NAVIGATION

(An explicit discussion of the navigation triangle.)

What does the sun's declination represent? It is *the exact distance* between the sun's tower and the North Pole — subtracted from 90°.

What does your latitude represent? It is *the exact distance* between your assumed position and the North Pole — subtracted from 90°.

What does your calculated height represent? It is *the exact distance* between the sun's tower and your assumed position — subtracted from 90°.

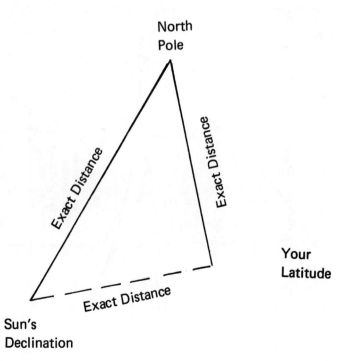

North Pole

Exact Distance

Exact Distance

Your Latitude

Exact Distance

Sun's Declination

You can make celestial navigation as concrete as possible. You are *always* dealing with exact distances over the surface of the earth — once you have pinpointed the base of the sun's tower.

Now, for a simple problem. Your noon latitude is N 32⁰ 00' and your approximate longitude is W 70⁰ 00'. You shoot the sun four hours and eight minutes after high noon and obtain:

Sextant: 35⁰ 00'   GMT 20:48   GHA 132⁰ 00'   DEC N 23⁰ 00'

In this problem the sun's declination is 23⁰ and your latitude is 32⁰. These two numbers determine the length of two legs of the triangle. One length is 90⁰ - 32⁰ = 58⁰ and the other is 90⁰ - 23⁰ = 67⁰. In terms of miles, the leg lengths are 58⁰ x 60' = 3,480 miles, and 67⁰ x 60' = 4,020 miles.

FROM HO 249:

LATITUDE   32⁰   Latitude Same Name As Declination

DEC 23⁰

LHA 62⁰   35⁰ 00'   +   24   83

                          Hc   d   Z

Solution of this triangle by look-up tables gives you a calculated height of 35⁰, and a Z value of 83⁰. The third leg length is 90⁰ - 35⁰ = 55⁰. (55⁰ x 60' = 3,300 miles.) The azimuth angle at your position is 360⁰ - 83⁰ = 277⁰

This triangle is the heart of celestial navigation. Your calculated height and observed height are measured distances of 3,300 nautical miles. Since your calculated height and observed height are the same distance from the base of the sun's tower *you must be at your assumed position.* (Next page)

Obviously, solving problems in celestial navigation does not require this type of exact mileage construction. We examined this problem to make it clear that you are not dealing with measurements that are "celestial" or "nebulous". You are working with the measurement of exact distances over the surface of the earth. When you shoot the sun you are *always* measuring the exact distance between you and the sun's tower.

Rather than use HO 249 to solve the triangle, you may use a hand held calculator to compute your position. The equations used to solve the triangle are:

$$\text{Sin(Hc)} = \text{Sin(Lat)} \times \text{Sin(Dec)} + \text{Cos(Lat)} \times \text{Cos(Dec)} \times \text{Cos(LHA)}$$

For Azimuth:

$$\text{Sin(Z)} = \text{Sin(LHA)} \times \frac{\text{Cos(Dec)}}{\text{Cos(Hc)}}$$

For resolving azimuth ambiguities:

$$\text{Cos LHA} = \frac{\text{Tan(Dec)}}{\text{Tan(Lat)}}$$

THE NAVIGATION TRIANGLE REPRESENTS EXACT DISTANCES ACROSS THE SURFACE OF THE EARTH

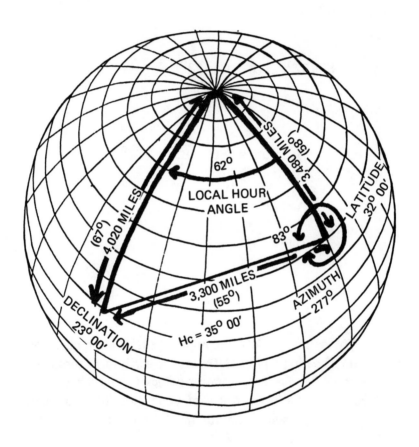

FOR EXAMPLE:

$Sin(Hc) = Sin(32^o) \times Sin(23^o) + Cos(32^o) \times Cos(23^o) \times Cos(62^o)$

$Hc = 35^o \ 00'$

$$Sin(Z) = Sin(62^o) \quad \times \quad \frac{Cos(23^o)}{Cos(35^o)}$$

$Z = 83^o$ Azimuth $= 360^o - 83^o = 277^o$

$$Cos(LHA) = \frac{Tan(23^o)}{Tan(32^o)}$$

$LHA = 47^o$

Three hours and eight minutes (47°) after high noon the sun's bearing will be 270°. As the earth turns through an angle of 47°, the sun's azimuth swings from 180° to 270°. Since the Local Hour Angle of your shot (62°) is greater than 47°, the sun's azimuth must be greater than 270°. Your correct azimuth is 277°.

WHAT IF I CANNOT ESTIMATE MY POSITION?

This legitimate question, asked by all beginners, is ignored by most books on celestial navigation. Put another way: You are placed somewhere in the world with a properly equipped yacht, but do not have *any* idea where you might be. What do you do?

The first step is to take your sextant out on deck and shoot the sun. Is the sun's height increasing? Yes! It must be morning. Continue shooting until high noon occurs. Note whether the sun passes to the north or south of you and record your sextant reading with the time that high noon occurred.

For example, you follow the above procedure and obtain:

Sextant: 85° 00′   GMT 21:02   DECEMBER 21, this year.
The sun passed to the north of your position.

Using this shot of the sun, you can accurately determine your latitude. Your longitude is determined by the time that high noon occurred; while not precise, it will give you a good assumed position. An hour later you shoot the sun and obtain:

Sextant: 75° 00′   GMT 22:02

This shot of the sun pinpoints your position, which is about 333 nautical miles south-west of a famous island.

Using the noon GMT, you can read your longitude directly from the almanac. You are obviously 5° south of the sun's latitude.

What is your latitude and longitude, and what is the name of the island which is on a bearing of 52°?

A "STAR TRACK" SEXTANT CHECK

(For Experts)

You, the worry wart, may ask the question: "How accurate is my sextant?" If banged or bumped, you may have reason to check its accuracy. The stars are separated by exact angles — which do not change over a lifetime. By measuring the known "track" or distance between two stars, you can verify the accuracy of your sextant.

The most identifiable constellation in the heavens is Orion. It is visible *throughout the world,* sometime during the night, for nine months of the year. You can use the two bright stars, above and below the belt, to check your sextant.

The distance between Rigel and Betelgeuse is 18° 36'. First measure the sextant's index error by using one of the stars. Then set your sextant for 18° 36'. By pointing at the lower star and aligning the sextant with the upper star, you should quickly see the second star. Adjust your sextant so both stars overlap. Read and record the value. Again check the sextant for index error.

You should read 18° 36' within 2' after removing the index error. Both stars should be at least 20° above the horizon. Refraction effects may cause these stars to appear closer by one or two minutes of angle.

Orion is not visible during May, June and July. Use Vega and Deneb if you are north of the equator and Antares and Spica if you are south of the equator. These stars will be visible when Orion is not available.

The above procedure is presented to assure you that your sextant is not disastrously in error.

ORION   BETELGEUSE & RIGEL   18° 36'
         VEGA & DENEB   23° 51'
         ANTARES & SPICA   45° 54'

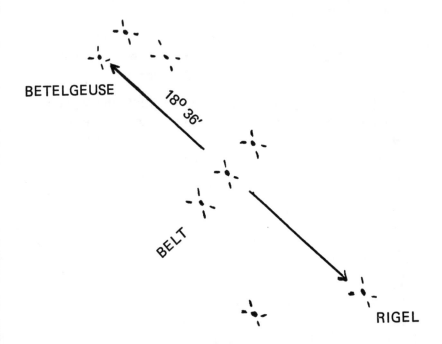

BETELGEUSE

180 36'

BELT

RIGEL

ORION CONSTELLATION

SUMMARY

There are three items that are peculiar to celestial navigation; a sextant, a Nautical Almanac and HO 249. The total cost of these items is less than $100. Are there any other world-wide navigation systems that cost less than this?

When you hear the wind in your sails and the rush of water against your boat, you are using this book as it is intended. You will make mistakes in working out your longitude shot — everyone does. The self-checking capability built into this book will enable you to catch, identify and correct your errors.

You will get your latitude on the first attempt. It is your choice whether you wish to measure your longitude by the simple check, or by the HO 249 technique.

If you have problems with the longitude shot, you can use a dog leg technique to approach your island. The latitude shot will be your *on course check,* while the longitude shot will give you the distance to your island. If you make an error in your longitude shot it will not matter; you will simply arrive sooner or later than expected — but *you will arrive.*

DEFINITION OF TERMS — PART 2

ABEAM This indicates an object is 90° to your heading.

ACCURACY Most sextants selling for more than $45 are capable of accuracies of better than one minute of angle. With good skill, and excellent sea conditions, you should be able to obtain a noon latitude accurate to within one nautical mile. As an estimate, you can expect two nautical miles error in your longitude shot.

ALMANAC If your Nautical Almanac is lost, HO 249 contains a "sun" almanac to the year 2000.

ASSUMED — Position. This is the position you select to enable you to use the HO 249 look-up table.

AVERAGE A single shot may be badly in error. Averaging will lessen the effects of one bad shot. A simple averaging procedure is to take three shots spaced one minute apart:

GMT	SEXTANT
19:41	44° 50'
19:42	
19:43	44° 30'

Let's say you missed your 19:42 shot. What would it have been? By inspection you can see it should have been 44° 40'. Now, let us supply the actual measurement for 19:42

19:42	44° 41'

Since 41' is close to 40', your 19:42 shot has been confirmed.

AZIMUTH   This is the sun's bearing, measured clockwise from true north.

CORR?   Is there an error in your watch? You may correct your watch reading at this point in the work form.

DR   Deduced Reckoning, also called dead reckoning. This is the process of predicting, or deducing, your position based on your speed and bearing from your last fix.

FIX   This is established by crossing two lines of position.

GHA   Greenwich Hour Angle. This is the position of the sun, measured westward from Greenwich, England. For angles from 0° to 180°, the GHA is equivalent to west longitudes. The GHA angles run from 0° to 360°. While not necessary for problems in celestial navigation, it is sometimes helpful to calculate the *east* longitude that the sun is on. Simply subtract the GHA from 360° to arrive at the east longitude.

$$GHA = 280^o$$
$$360^o - 280^o = E\ 80^o\ 00'\ Longitude$$

HO 249   A set of three books which covers celestial navigation for the entire world. Book one specializes in star navigation. Books two and three covers all objects; stars, sun, moon and planets. HO stands for *Hydrographic Office,* and 249 is the number of the publication.

INTERPOLATION – This is the process of finding an in between value.

1	2	3	4	5
15	20		30	35

What value should be under the 3? In this case, obviously, 25. This is the process you use to find minutes of calculated height when you are given minutes of declination.

LHA   Local Hour Angle. This is the difference between your longitude and the sun's longitude. It is always measured westward from your longitude.

MISTAKES   The work form is designed to remind you to carry plus and minus signs. In addition, all values obtained from the tables are directly entered in the log, making later checking simple. Any serious disagreement between your DR position and your fix should cause you to recheck your work.

NORTH   True north and magnetic north. All bearings given in celestial navigation are referred to *true* north. Lines of longitude run true north and true south. Your magnetic compass will indicate magnetic headings. The numerical difference between true and magnetic bearings (magnetic variation) will be shown on your chart.

RADIO   Time. The time beeps heard on AM or FM radio stations are accurate to within two seconds. This is sufficiently accurate for use in celestial navigation. If you have a short-wave radio receiver, you may listen to WWV. This is a GMT time transmitting station broadcasting on 2.5, 5.0, 10.0, 15.0, 20.0, 25.0 and 30.0 mega-hertz. This station can be heard anywhere in the world, sometime during the day, on one of these frequencies.

SUN'S – Position. This is the base of the sun's tower whose coordinates, at any instant of time, are given by the Nautical Almanac.

TRIPLE – Checking.   The shots you make — morning, noon and afternoon — result in three Lines of Position. Plotting the resulting LOP's on a map will form a "cocked hat", an excellent way to check your work. Use of this technique will confirm the accuracy of all three Lines of Position. If the resulting Lines of Position fall within five miles of each other, you have achieved a reasonable degree of accuracy in the use of your sextant. Advance your Lines of Position — as required.

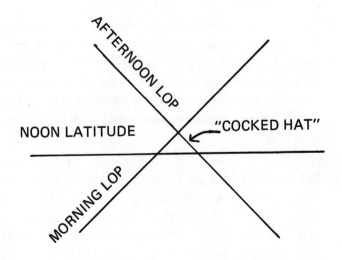

TIME – Corrections. By checking your watch against radio time, you will know how many seconds your watch is in error. Your watch may be corrected in the space provided in the work form. An incorrect time will displace your position east or west. If you find that your watch was slow or fast, *after* you have plotted your position, you may use the following TIME/LONGITUDE correction form.

WATCH **24** SECONDS FAST (SLOW) ÷ 4 = **6 '**

LONGITUDE
CORRECTION

+72° 34'   **+6'**   =   **W 72° 40'**

Plotted Longitude   Minus if Fast   Time Corrected
(Plus for West)   (Plus if Slow)   Longitude
Minus for East

VERNIER   The $20 sextant has a vernier scale for reading minutes of angle. This scale reading technique is added complexity in the use of the sextant. The EBBCO and higher priced sextants use a worm gear to "finely divide" the degree scale, thus obviating the need for a vernier scale. The literature supplied with the less expensive sextant adequately describes the use of a vernier scale.

WATCH   Accurate time for small boats used to mean a high priced chronometer. With the advent of digital (crystal) watches, this problem has been solved. The liquid crystal watch, selling for about $25 is accurate to within 15 seconds per month. This watch will meet your time keeping needs.

SUN, MOON, (PLANETS,) STARS

2 Object: _Venus_

Sextant: _15° 33'_

I. E. _+ 6'_

Height-of-Eye _- 3'_

Sun, Moon (5) _- 3'_

(Refraction)

Total: Ho _15° 33'_

1 Deduced Position _N 32° 00'_ Latitude

Date _Dec. 2, 1980_

Day _Tuesday_

GMT _8:00:00_

Corr? _N 35° 00'_ Longitude

GMT _8:00:00_

From the Nautical Almanac

3 Dec. _S13° 13'_ GMT Hour _8:_ GHA _332° 57'_

Minutes, Seconds _00:00_ (+) _0° 00'_

"d" _6_ "v" _____ H. P. ____

Dec. _S 13° 13'_ GMT: _8:00:00_ GHA _332° 57'_ (+360) 1.

4

Greenwich Hour Angle .... GHA: _332° 57'_

Assumed Longitude .... _W 34° 57'_ 2.

TOTAL: Local Hour Angle _298° 00_

(-360) 3.

Local Hour Angle .... _298°_

ADJUST

---

5 Assumed Position: Latitude _N 32°_ Longitude _W 34° 57'_

---

6 HEIGHT AND BEARING USING HO 249

Declination Latitude (Assumed)

_298_ _S 13° 13'_ Same (Contrary) _N 32° 00'_

Local Hour Angle

---

7 Interpolation Table Bearing 4.

Dec. _S 13°_ Hc _15° 35'_ 360

(d = _37_) X _13'_ /60= _- 8'_ (Z= _117°_) Subtract if Your LHA is less than 180°

Dec. _S 13° 13'_ Hc _15° 27'_

Ho & Hc Comparison Ho = _15° 33'_ Hc = _15° 27'_ (Towards) Away (Difference)

_6'_

8 HoMoTo

CHAPTER V

THE MOON, PLANETS AND STARS

The prerequisite for this chapter is one month celestial navigation *at sea*. As you build capability and confidence with sun shots, you can begin preparing for navigation with these remaining celestial objects. Reducing these objects is not difficult. By slightly modifying the sun work form you can deal with these additional celestial bodies. Your best approach is to examine the differences between the Sun Work Form and the work form for the Sun, Moon, Planets and Stars. (Previous page.)

Before dawn on Tuesday, December 2, 1980, you plan to check your position. You are sailing due west at five knots. Your DR position is: N 32° 00' and W 35° 00'.

You shoot Venus which lies to the southeast and Regulus which lies to the south. You read:

Venus: Sextant 15° 33'   GMT 8:00:00   I.E. +6'
Regulus: Sextant 69° 00'   GMT 8:05:51   I.E. +3'

You fix your position by reducing these shots and plotting the resulting Lines of Position on your chart. As the first light of dawn appears in the east, you pinpoint your position as:

N 32° 16' and W 34° 40'

HOW DO I REDUCE A PLANET SHOT?

The reduction of the planet Venus is almost identical to the sun reduction. Since a planet does not have semi-diameter, you need only correct your sextant reading for refraction. This value, – 3', is found on the same page the sun's SD and refraction value was found. (next page.)

The position of the stars and planets is found on the left hand daily page of the Nautical Almanac. The Greenwich Hour Angle and declination for Venus is listed exactly as the sun was listed. You find:

$$\text{Venus: GHA } 332^\circ \ 57' \quad \text{DEC. S } 13^\circ \ 13'$$

The work form asks for "d" and "v" corrections. Normally you can ignore these corrections for planets. The stars do not require this correction. The moon always requires this correction. These corrections will be fully discussed during the moon shot.

The rest of the reduction is identical to the sun shot, except for the azimuth determination. (Previous page.)

1. If your LHA is between 180° and 360° you use the "Z" value directly.

2. If your LHA is between 0° and 180°, you subtract the "Z" value from 360° to obtain your actual azimuth.

(If you are south of the equator, you must use the azimuth footnote (4) on the pictorial work form, page 108)

From this sight reduction you obtain a bearing of 117° and an intercept value of 6' towards.

STARS AND PLANETS

App. Alt.	Corrⁿ
14 16	−3·7
14 40	−3·6
15 04	
15 30	
15 57	−3·4
16 26	
16 56	−3·2
17 28	−3·1
18 02	−3·0
18 38	−2·9
19 17	−2·8

FRONT COVER:

NAUTICAL ALMANAC

DAILY PAGE

1980 December 2, 3, 4 (Tues., Wed., Thurs.)

G.M.T.	ARIES G.H.A.	VENUS −3.4 G.H.A.	Dec.		STARS Name	S.H.A.	Dec.
d h	o ′	o ′	o ′			o ′	o ′
2 00	70 59.3	213 01.7	S13 05.2				
01	86 01.7	228 01.1	06.2		Regulus	208 09.8	N12 03.7
02	101 04.2	243 00.6	07.2		Rigel		
03	116 06.7	258 00.1 ··	08.2		Rigil Kent.	140 26.2	S60 45.0
04	131 09.1	272 59.5	09.2		Sabik	102 41.4	S15 42.0
05	146 11.6	287 59.0	10.2				
06	161 14.1	302 58.5	S13 11.2		Schedar	350 08.5	N56 26.1
07	176 16.5	317 57.9	12.2		Shaula	96 56.0	S37 05.3
08	191 19.0	332 57.3	13.2		Sirius	258 55.3	S16 41.4
09	206 21.4	347 56.8	14.2		Spica	158 57.6	S11 03.5
10	221 23.9	2 56.3	15.2		Suhail	223 10.5	S43 21.1
11	236 26.4	17 55.7	16.2				

HOW DO I REDUCE A STAR SHOT?

The star reduction is almost identical to the planet reduction. Since all stars are fixed and unmoving, one standard "longitude" reference has been chosen, called the "First Point of Aries". The angle of a star westward from this reference point is called the star's siderial hour angle (SHA). The Greenwich Hour Angle of Aries is listed on the left hand daily page of the Nautical Almanac. (See previous page.)

The declinations of the stars do not change, and can be taken directly from the Nautical Almanac and entered in the work form. The Siderial Hour Angle of Regulus is $208^{\circ} 10'$. This value is entered on the star table found on the pictorial work form. (Overleaf)

Siderial Hour Angle: (SHA)	$208^{\circ} 10'$	
Greenwich Hour Angle: (GHA Aries)	$191^{\circ} 19'$ (add)	
GHA of Regulus	$399^{\circ} 29'$	
(is the GHA Greater than 360°?)	$- 360^{\circ} 00'$ (sub.)	
GHA of Regulus:	$39^{\circ} 29'$	

The GHA of Aries is $191^{\circ} 19'$ at 8:00:00. (prev. page) The SHA of Regulus is added to the GHA of Aries to obtain $399^{\circ} 29'$. Because this is greater than 360° you subtract 360° and obtain $39^{\circ} 29'$.

From this point on, the calculations are identical to the planet reduction. Regulus' intercept and bearing are 19' away, on a bearing of 197°. This line of position crosses the venus line and fixes your position as N $32^{\circ} 16'$ and W $34^{\circ} 40'$. (Overleaf)

SUN, MOON, PLANETS (STARS)

2 Object: _Regulus_
Sextant: 69° 00'
I. E. + 3'
Height-of-Eye - 3'
Sun, Moon (5) 0'
(Refraction)
Total: Ho 69° 00'

1 Deduced Position N32°00'
Date _Dec. 2, 1980_ Latitude
Day _Tuesday_
GMT 8:05:51
Corr? 0.00 W35°00'
GMT 8.05.51 Longitude
— From the Nautical Almanac

3
Dec. N12°04' GMT Hour 8.
Minutes, Seconds 05:51 (+) 1° 28'
GHA 39°29'

"d" _____ "v" _____ H. P. _____

Dec. N12°04' GMT: 8:05:51 GHA 40° 57'
(+360) 1.

4
Greenwich Hour Angle .... GHA: 40° 57'
Assumed Longitude .... 34° 57' 2.
TOTAL: Local Hour Angle 6° 00'
(-360) 3.

Local Hour Angle .... 6° 00'

ADJUST

5 Assumed Position: Latitude N32° Longitude W34°57'

6 HEIGHT AND BEARING USING HO 249

Declination Latitude (Assumed)

6° N 12°04' (Same) Contrary N 32° 00'
Local Hour Angle

7 Interpolation Table Bearing **4.**
Dec. N12° (Hc 69°15') 360
d + 58' X 04 /60=+ 04 Z= 163° Subtract if
Dec N12°04' Hc 69° 19° 197° Your LHA is less
than 180°

Ho & Hc Hc = 69° 19'
Comparison Ho = 69° 00'
19' Towards
(Away) (Difference)

8 HoMoTo

Star Table

Star's SHA = $208°$ 10'
GHA Aries = $191°$ 19' ADD
___
Star's GHA = $399°$ 29'
___
(-360)
(Star's GHA) = $39°$ 29'
___

Moon Table (5)

Sex- ($56°$ 29')
tant ... 41.8'
H.P. 54.1 ... 2.6'
___
Lower Limb ... 44.4'
(-30' ?)
(Upper Limb) ... 14.4'

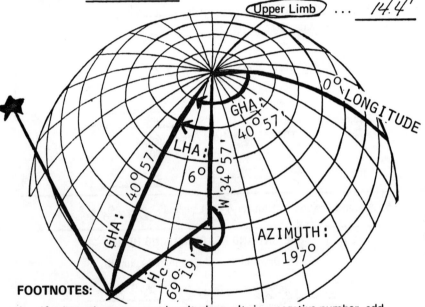

FOOTNOTES:

1. If subtracting your west longitude results in a negative number, add 360° to the Greenwich Hour Angle.

2. Subtract the longitude if West. Add Longitude if east.

3. If the Local Hour Angle is greater than 360°, subtract 360° from the Local Hour Angle.

4. If south of the equator, use the following bearing calculations:

If your LHA is between
180° - 360°:

     180°

Z = _____ Subtract

If your LHA is between
0° - 180°:

     180°

Z = _____ Add

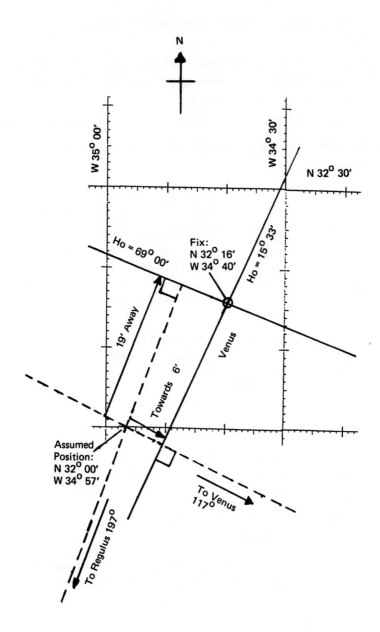

HOW DO I REDUCE THE MOON SHOT?

Later, in the morning, you shoot the Moon as it passes to the south of you. Since you cannot see the lower limb, you shoot the upper limb and obtain:

Sextant: 56° 29′ GMT 10:30 i.e. − 11′ upper limb

The corrections for your sextant readings are similar to your sun corrections:

Sextant	56° 29′	
I.E.	− 11′	"on arc"
Hgt-of-Eye	− 3′	
Refraction	− 1′	
Semi-Diameter	− 15′	U.L.
Parallax	+ 30′	
Ho	56° 29′	

Subtract if upper limb:
H.P. X Cos (Sextant)

The fact that the moon is much closer to the earth than other celestial objects causes a parallax problem, and this requires a parallax correction.

$$\frac{\text{Parallax}}{\text{Correction}} = \text{H.P. X Cos (Sextant)}$$
(Where H.P. is the Horizontal Parallax)

Looking at the daily page in the Nautical Almanac, (next page) you find a H.P. value of 54.1′, and a semi-diameter value of 14.7′

Parallax = 54.1 X Cos (56° 29′)
Parallax = 29.9′

Adding up all these corrections gives you an observed height of 56° 29′, which is entered in the work form.

NAUTICAL ALMANAC   DAILY PAGE

1980 DECEMBER 2, 3, 4 (TUES., WED., THURS.)

G.M.T.	SUN		MOON					
	G.H.A.	Dec.	G.H.A.	v	Dec.	d	H.P.
d h	° ′	° ′	° ′	′	° ′	′	′
2 00	182 39.6	S21 56.7	241 44.2	15.7	N 0 31.8	10.3	54.2
01	197 39.4	57.1	256 18.9	15.8	0 21.5	10.2	54.2
02	212 39.2	57.5	270 53.7	15.7	0 11.3	10.2	54.1
03	227 38.9 ··	57.8	285 28.4	15.8	N 0 01.1	10.3	54.1
04	242 38.7	58.2	300 03.2	15.8	S 0 09.2	10.2	54.1
05	257 38.4	58.6	314 38.0	15.7	0 19.4	10.2	54.1
06	272 38.2	S21 58.9	329 12.7	15.8	S 0 29.6	10.3	54.1
07	287 38.0	59.3	343 47.5	15.8	0 39.9	10.2	54.1
08	302 37.7	21 59.7	358 22.3	15.7	0 50.1	10.2	54.1
09	317 37.5	22 00.0					54.1
10	332 37.2	00.4	27 31.8	15.8	1 10.5	10.3	54.1
11	347 37.0	00.8					
	S.D. 16.3	d 0.3	S.D. 14.7		14.7		14.8

YELLOW PAGE

30ᵐ INCREMENTS AND CORRECTIONS

30ᵐ	SUN PLANETS	ARIES	MOON	v or Corrⁿ d		v or Corrⁿ d		v or Corrⁿ d	
s	° ′	° ′	° ′	′	′	′	′	′	′
00	7 30·0	7 31·2	7 09·5	3·5	1·8	9·5	4·8	15·5	7·9
01	7 30·3	7 31·5	7 09·7	3·6	1·8	9·6	4·9	15·6	7·9
02	7 30·5	7 31·7	7 10·0	3·7	1·9	9·7	4·9		
03	7 30·8	7 32·0	7 10·2	3·8	1·9	9·8	5·0	15·8	8·0
04	7 31·0	7 32·2	7 10·5	3·9	2·0	9·9	5·0		
05	7 31·3	7 32·5	7 10·7	4·0	2·0	10·0	5·1	16·0	8·1
06	7 31·5	7 32·7	7 10·9	4·1	2·1	10·1	5·1	16·1	8·2
07	7 31·8	7 33·0	7 11·2	4·2	2·1			16·2	8·2
08	7 32·0	7 33·2	7 11·4	4·3	2·2	10·3	5·2	16·3	8·3
09	7 32·3	7 33·5	7 11·6	4·4	2·2			16·4	8·3

THE "d" AND "v" CORRECTIONS

The moon's Greenwich Hour Angle and Declination change rapidly between the positions listed, hour by hour, in the Nautical Almanac. To find the position of the moon at the time of your shot, you must interpolate. The interpolation table is part of the "Increments and Correction" table. The "d" and "v" values obtained from the daily page are: (Previous page)

"d" = 10.3'   "v" = 15.8'   H.P. = 54.1'

When you look up the correction for thirty minutes of time, (7° 9.5') you also look up the amount by which the GHA and DEC. of the moon change in 1/2 hour.

Since you shot the moon thirty minutes after the hour, your corrections will be 1/2 the "d" and "v" values. The "d" correction is 5.2', and the "v" correction is 8.0'. (See next page.) The declination of the moon at 10:30 is S 1° 15'.

The H.P. value appears with the "d" and "v" values and is written down at this point in the work form.

The remainder of the work form is completed in the same manner as the sun shot. An intercept value of 16' is obtained which gives you a latitude of N 32° 16'.

To check your longitude, you shoot the sun and obtain:

Sextant: 15° 34'   GMT: 10 : 36 : 00   I.E. - 10'

This shot confirms your longitude which is:

W 34° 55'

SUN, (MOON,) PLANETS, STARS

2 Object: *Moon - Upper Limb*
Sextant: *56° 29'*
I. E. *– 11'*
Height-of-Eye *– 03'*
Sun (Moon) 5, *+ 14'*
Refraction
Total: Ho *56° 29'*

1 Deduced Position *N 32° 16'* Latitude
Date *Dec 2, 1980*
Day *Tuesday*
GMT *10.30.00* *W 34° 55'* ➤➤
Corr?
GMT *10.30.00* Longitude
—— From the Nautical Almanac

3
Dec. *51° 10'* GMT Hour *10.* GHA *27° 32'*
Minutes, Seconds *30.00* (+) *7° 09'*
"d" + *10.3* + *5.2* "v" + *15.8* + *08* H. P. *54.1*
Dec. *51° 15'* GMT: *10.30.00* GHA *34° 49'*
(+360) **1.**

4
Greenwich Hour Angle . . . . GHA: *34° 49'*
Assumed Longitude . . . . *34° 49'* **2.**
TOTAL: Local Hour Angle *0° 00'*
(-360) **3.**
Local Hour Angle . . . . *0° 00'*

ADJUST

5 Assumed Position: Latitude *N 32* Longitude *W 34° 49'*

6 HEIGHT AND BEARING USING HO 249

Declination   Latitude (Assumed)
                         Same
0°   *S 1° 15'* (Contrary) *N* *32°*
Local Hour Angle

7 Interpolation Table   Bearing **4.**
Dec. *51*   (Hc *57° 00'*)   360
d – *60*) X *15* /60 = – *15* (Z = *180°*) Subtract if
Dec *51° 15'*   Hc *56° 45'*   *180°*   Your LHA is less than 180°

Ho & Hc   Hc = *56° 45'*
Comparison   Ho = *56° 29'*
                                    Towards
                16'   (Away) (Difference)

8 HoMoTo

THE NAUTICAL ALMANAC
PARALLAX CORRECTION

The Nautical Almanac uses a different table and technique for the moon's refraction, semi-diameter and parallax correction. For example:

Sextant	56° 29'
I. E.	− 11' "On Arc"
Hgt−of−Eye	− 3'
Moon Table (5)	+ 14'
Ho	56° 29'

Using the moon table (5) on page 108, you calculate the correction for these three values.

(5) Moon Table

Refraction	− 1'		
Semi−Diameter	− 15'	(Sextant 56° 29')	41.8'
Parallax	+ 30'	H. P. 54.1	2.6'
Total	+ 14'	Lower Limb	44.4'
			(− 30.0' ?)
		Upper Limb	14.4'

The first table is entered with the sextant's height. (App. Alt.) The value obtained, 41.8', is entered in the moon table. Using the H.P. value you obtained from the daily page, and the fact you shot the upper limb, you obtain a second correction of 2.6'. The total of these two values is 44.4'. Since you shot the upper limb, you must subtract 30' from 44.4'. The result, 14.4', is the correction for the lower limb. This value is rounded off and entered in the work form. You now have two independent means to calculate the moon's refraction, semi-diameter, and parallax value.

NAUTICAL ALMANAC: Back cover

ALTITUDE CORRECTION TABLES 35° - 90° — MOON

App. Alt.	35°-39° Corrⁿ	40°-44° Corrⁿ	45°-49° Corrⁿ	50°-54° Corrⁿ	55°-59° Corrⁿ
00	35 56·5	40 53·7	45 50·5	50 46·9	55 43·1
10	56·4	53·6	50·4	46·8	42·9
20	56·3	53·5	50·2	46·7	42·8
30	56·2	53·4	50·1	46·5	42·7
40	56·2	53·3	50·0	46·4	42·5
50	56·1	53·2	49·9	46·3	42·4
00	36 56·0	41 53·1	46 49·8	51 46·2	56 42·3
10	55·9	53·0	49·7	46·0	42·1
20	55·8	52·8	49·5	45·9	42·0
30	55·7	52·7	49·4	45·8	41·8
40	55·6	52·6	49·3	45·7	41·7
50	55·5	52·5	49·2	45·5	41·6
00	37 55·4	42 52·4	47 49·1	52 45·4	57 41·4
10	55·3	52·3	49·0	45·3	41·3
20	55·2	52·2	48·8	45·2	41·2
30	55·1	52·1	48·7	45·0	41·0
40	55·0	52·0	48·6	44·9	40·9
50	55·0	51·9	48·5	44·8	40·8

H.P.	L U	L U	L U	L U	L U
54·0	1·1 1·7	1·3 1·9	1·5 2·1	1·7 2·4	2· 2·6
54·3	1·4 1·8	1·6 2·0	1·8 2·2	2·0 2·5	2·3 2·7
54·6	1·7 2·0	1·9 2·2	2·1 2·4	2·3 2·6	2·5 2·8
54·9	2·0 2·2	2·2 2·3	2·3 2·5	2·5 2·7	2·7 2·9
55·2	2·3 2·3	2·5 2·4	2·6 2·6	2·8 2·8	3·0 2·9

HOW DO I USE THE MOON SHOT?

The second easiest object to identify and shoot is the moon. It is visible during daylight for about ten days out of thirty. Sun–Moon shots are worthwhile as a learning experience, and as a means to quickly fix your position. The best time to do this is during a high noon shot, with the moon to the east or west of you. Alternatively, you may calculate the meridian pass for the moon, and shoot the sun for your longitude.

HOW DO I SHOOT THE PLANETS AND STARS?

Shooting a star or planet requires that both the object and the horizon be visible at the same time. This condition exists for about 30 minutes after sunset, and 30 minutes before sunrise.

PLANET IDENTIFICATION

The meridian pass for the planets is listed on the daily page for all four visible planets. (Lower right hand corner.) At the time of meridian pass the planets will be due north or due south. By looking for them at this time, you should be able to locate and identify them.

STAR IDENTIFICATION

The stars that are easiest to identify and shoot are Betelgeuse and Rigel in the constellation Orion. The other stars take a considerable amount of work to identify and shoot. A star identification chart is provided in the Nautical Almanac for this purpose.

DEFINITION OF TERMS — PART 3

First Point of Aries: This is a standard reference point on the celestial sphere. It is the point where the sun crosses the celestial equator on March 21. (The first day of spring.)

Azimuth Equation: HO 249 has an azimuth equation printed on each page. It is the same equation used in the work form.

Celestial Sphere: An imaginary sphere which circles the earth once every 23 hours and 56 minutes. The stars are "imbedded" in the celestial sphere. The north star is at the axis of this sphere. The sphere turns around this point.

"d" A small incremental (or decremental) adjustment in the declination of an object.

HO 229: This is a series of six books of "look-up" tables similar to HO 249.

HO 249, Volume 1: This book is designed for star shots alone. If you plan to execute more than 50 star shots, buy the book. Otherwise, use Volumes II and III for star shots. (Over half the stars have declinations from N 30° to S 30°, which may be used with Volumes II and III.)

Intercept: The difference between your observed and calculated height is called the "intercept".

North (Pole) Star: Polarus is unique because it is almost directly over the North Pole. If it were directly over the pole you could shoot the star and read your latitude from your sextant. The star is about one degree away from the pole. The Nautical Almanac has a table in the back of the book for calculating your latitude from Polarus. (The star requires a sextant with good optics to find and shoot.)

DEFINITION OF TERMS — PART 3 (continued)

Parallax: This refers to the non-parallism of light rays from the moon. If you are directly under the moon, the parallax correction is zero.

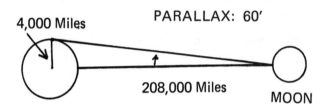

EARTH (Viewed from above the North Pole.)

If the moon is on the horizon, you will require a parallax correction of about 60'.

Star Magnitudes: The brightness of the stars and planets is given in magnitudes.

1. The planet Venus will occasionally have a magnitude of – 4.

2. The bright star, Sirus, has a magnitude of – 1.6.

3. The magnitude of the North Star is +2.0.

4. The dimmest star you can see has a magnitude of + 6.0.

SHA: The Siderial Hour Angle of a star is measured westward from a standard reference called the first point of Aries.

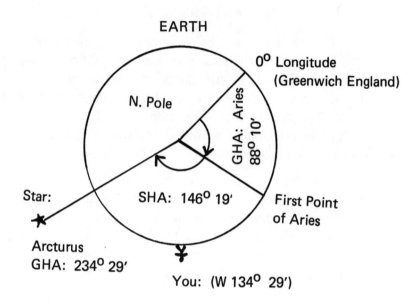

For example, using the star Arcturus:

	GHA Aries:	88° 10′
+	SHA Arcturus:	146° 19′
	GHA Arcturus:	234° 29′
−	Assumed Longitude:	134° 29′
	LHA Arcturus:	100° 00′

Arcturus is 100 degrees to the west of your position.

Tropic of Cancer: The farthest north the sun gets.
(N 23° 26′ on June 21)

Tropic of Capricorn: The farthest south the sun gets.
(S 23° 26′ on December 21)

"**v**": A small incremental correction, or adjustment, in the Greenwich Hour Angle of an object.

THE ARTIFICIAL HORIZON

The noon shot can be easily reduced from the deck of your sailboat. The afternoon shot requires practice. It may be more convenient for you to shoot and reduce the afternoon sun at home. You need one additional item — a bucket of water. The bucket should be indoors, protected from any draft. The principle is simple; if the sun is 30° above the horizon, its reflected image will be 30° below the horizon.

The procedure is to get the sun, and the sun's reflection, to overlap in your sextant. You do this by looking through the sextant at the bucket of water, observing the sun's reflection in the water. Moving the arm of your sextant you find the real sun and cause the two to overlay. You read the sun's height as 60° 13'. You measure the sextant's index error as 13' "on arc".

Sextant:	60° 13'
I.E.	− 13'
Reflected Height :	60° 00'
Divided by two:	30° 00'
Refraction :	− 2'
Observed Height (Ho)	29° 58'

Since you measured the height of the sun from its center, you do not correct for semi-diameter. The only additional correction is for refraction, which you obtain from the Nautical Almanac. Now, use your observed height for a normal sight reduction.

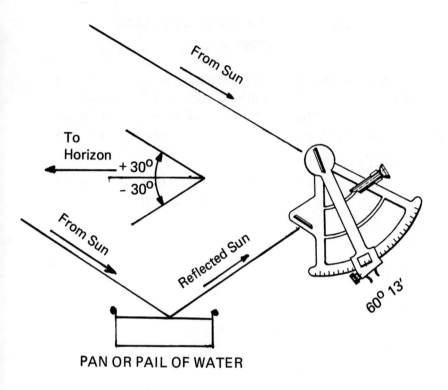

To Horizon

+ 30°
− 30°

From Sun

From Sun

Reflected Sun

60° 13'

PAN OR PAIL OF WATER

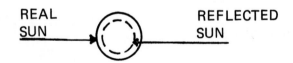

REAL SUN

REFLECTED SUN

THE REAL AND REFLECTED SUN ARE
CONCENTRIC WHEN THE ARM OF THE SEXTANT
IS PROPERLY ADJUSTED

ANSWERS TO PRACTICE PROBLEMS
(Page 38)

In these problems you are maintaining an approximate speed of 5 knots on a heading of 135° and 90° true. Assume that you read a "Distance Run" of 5.4 miles on your log between the time of your noon shot and the time of your afternoon shot.

Your advanced noon latitude will be four nautical miles south of your noon latitude for the shots you made on the 17th, 18th, 19th and 20th.

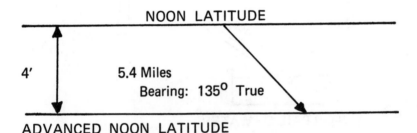

NOON LATITUDE

4'   5.4 Miles
      Bearing: 135° True

ADVANCED NOON LATITUDE

Your noon latitudes will be identical to the latitudes given here. The Simple Longitude Check was calculated as described in Chapter 2. The afternoon longitude is established by advancing the noon latitude and crossing it with the afternoon Line of Position.

YOUR POSITION IS ESTABLISHED
BY SUN SHOTS

Date:	Your Noon Latitude:	The Simple Longitude Check:	Your Afternoon Longitude:
6/17	N 36° 53′	W 75° 45′	W 75° 40′
6/1!	N 35° 25′	W 74° 00′	W 73° 52′
6/19	N 33° 56′	W 72° 15′	W 72° 05′
6/20	N 32° 26′	W 70° 15′	W 70° 03′
6/21	N 32° 18′	W 67° 30′	W 67° 28′
6/22	N 32° 16′	W 65° 30′	W 65° 23′

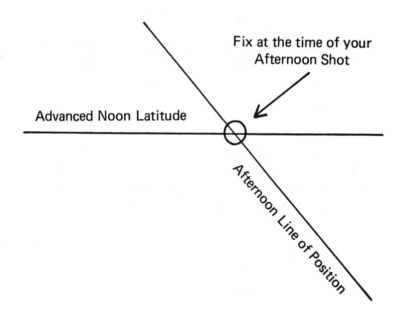

Fix at the time of your
Afternoon Shot

Advanced Noon Latitude

Afternoon Line of Position

YOUR OBJECTIVES

Your goal in reading this book is to get from point "A" to point "B". You can quickly gain the intellectual concepts necessary to navigate across an ocean by reading Chapter I. If you are prepared with the proper concepts, *you will* master celestial navigation.

Sextant use on a small boat can range from easy in good weather, to arduous in heavy weather. Your accuracy with a sextant will improve rapidly with familiarity and use. After three or four days of shooting, you will have confidence that your measured latitude is within two nautical miles of the correct latitude.

Your longitude shooting, because of the complexity, will be more error prone. The simple longitude check, while less accurate, is more reliable because of its simplicity.

My experience, in teaching this course, is that individuals with no experience can solve the major problems in this book with five hours of study. Without an instructor this may take longer, since you proceed at your own pace.

I wish to offer my congratulations to you on your entry into the fraternity of celestial navigators. Your departure on a voyage of a thousand miles, with confidence in your ability to pinpoint your position, will be the most satisfying achievement of your sailing career.

THE LATITUDE SHOT

Date _____   Day _____

Latitude: _____   Longitude _____

PREDICTING HIGH NOON

Meridian Pass . . . .   _____

Longitude: Add time if west   _____

                   Sub. time if east

        This is the GMT of High Noon: _____

        Convert to Local Time: _____

     This is the local time of High Noon

PREDICTING "HEIGHT OF SUN"

                $90°$ Degrees

LATITUDE: _____   (Subtract)

                    Height of Celestial Equator

                    Add Dec. if north

DECLINATION: _____   Subtract Dec. if south (1)

                    Calculated Height (Hc) (2)

SEXTANT MEASUREMENTS

SEXTANT READING . . . .   _____

                 Subtract if "ON ARC"

INDEX ERROR: Add if "OFF ARC"   _____

HEIGHT OF EYE (DIP) . . . .   _____

SEMI-DIAMETER AND REFRACTION . . . .   _____

     TOTAL: OBSERVED HEIGHT (Ho)

Ho & Hc Comparison

            _____   Towards

     Ho Mo To   Away (Difference)

1. If south of equator; add Dec. if south, subtract if north.
2. If Hc is greater than $90°$, subtract from $180°$.

A SIMPLE LATITUDE CHECK

90° 00'	=	89° 60'	
OBSERVED HEIGHT	=	_____	(SUBTRACT)

DISTANCE FROM TOWER	=		
SUN'S DECLINATION	=		(ADD IN SUMMER) (SUBTRACT IN WINTER)

YOUR LATITUDE IS: _____

A SIMPLE LONGITUDE CHECK

MORNING SEXTANT :_____ TIME : _____

AFTERNOON SEXTANT :_____ TIME : _____

DIFFERENCE : _____

DIFFERENCE DIVIDED BY TWO : _____

ACTUAL HIGH NOON : _____

LONGITUDE : _____ PREDICTED NOON : _____

ACTUAL NOON WAS : EARLY .
LATE : _____ (Minutes of Time)

X 15

PLUS IF LATE
MINUS IF EARLY _____ (Minutes of Longitude)

Predicted Longitude: PLUS FOR WEST
MINUS FOR EAST _____ (Degrees of Longitude)

YOUR LONGITUDE IS: _____ (TOTAL)

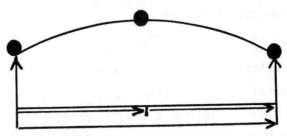

SUN

2   Sextant Observations   **1**   Deduced Position

Sextant: _____   Date _____
                                                      _____ Latitude
I.E. _____   Day _____
Height-of-Eye _____   GMT _____
SD & Refraction_____   Corr? _____
                                                      _____ Longitude
Total: Ho = _____   GMT _____

3   **SUN'S POSITION – From the Nautical Almanac**

Dec. _____   GMT
                         Hour _____   GHA _____
          Minutes, Seconds_____   (+) _____

Dec.   GMT: GHA:
                                                 (+ 360)   1.

4   Local Hour Angle = GHA +/- Longitude
Greenwich Hour Angle . . . . GHA: _____
Assumed Longitude . . . . _____ 2.
                    TOTAL: Local Hour Angle_____
                                                 (–360)   3.
Local Hour Angle . . . .

---

5 Assumed Position: Latitude   Longitude

---

6   Find the Sun's Height and Bearing Using HO 249
                    Sun's Declination   Latitude (Assumed)
                                          Same
_____ ⌐ _____ Contrary ⌐ _____
Local Hour Angle

---

7   Sun's Hc Interpolation Table   Sun's Bearing   4.
Dec. _____   Hc _____   360
                                                  Z =   Morning
d _____ X ___ /60= _____   Azimuth
                                                           Afternoon
Dec. _____   Hc _____   Azimuth

Ho & Hc
Comparison
                    _____   Towards
                                                 Away (Difference)
8   HoMoTo

ADJUST

SUN, MOON, PLANETS, STARS

ADJUST

(1) Deduced Position

Latitude:

Longitude:

Date

Day

GMT

Corr?

GMT

(2) Object:

Sextant:

I.E.

Height-of-Eye

Sun, Moon (5)

Refraction

Total: Ho

(3) Nautical Almanac:

Dec.   Hour   GHA

                              (+)

"d"   Minutes, Seconds

Dec.   GMT   GHA   "v"

                              (+ 360)   H.P.

(4) Greenwich Hour Angle . . . .   GHA: 1.

Assumed Longitude . . . .   2.

                              (− 360)   3.

TOTAL: Local Hour Angle

Local Hour Angle

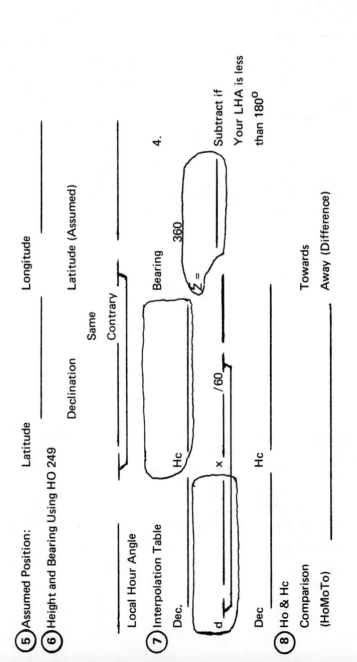

5 Assumed Position: Latitude _____   Longitude _____

6 Height and Bearing Using HO 249

    Declination _____   Latitude (Assumed) _____

    Same

    Contrary

Local Hour Angle _____

7 Interpolation Table

Dec. _____   Hc _____   Bearing _____   4.

    d _____   x _____   / 60

    Dec _____   Hc _____   Z = _____ 360

8 Ho & Hc

    Comparison   Towards

    (HoMoTo) _____   Away (Difference)

Subtract if

Your LHA is less

than 180°

Star Table   **Moon Table (5)**

Star's SHA =   Sex -

GHA Aries =   ADD   tant   ... _____

_____   H.P. _____ ... _____

Star's GHA =   _____

(-360)   Lower Limb ... _____

Star's GHA =   (-30' ?)

_____   Upper Limb ... _____

FOOTNOTES:

1. If subtracting your west longitude results in a negative number, add 360° to the Greenwich Hour Angle.

2. Subtract the longitude if West. Add Longitude if east.

3. If the Local Hour Angle is greater than 360°, subtract 360° from the Local Hour Angle.

4. If south of the equator, use the following bearing calculations:

If your LHA is between   If your LHA is between
180° - 360°:   0° - 180°:

    180°   180°

Z = _____ Subtract   Z = _____ Add

INDEX